Christmas *with* COUNTRY LIVING

Volume VI

Text by Debra Muller Price

Hearst Communications, Inc.

Christmas with Country Living *Volume VI*

Oxmoor House, Inc.
Book Division of Southern Progress Corporation
P.O. Box 2463, Birmingham, AL 35201

ISBN: 0-8487-2532-8
ISSN: 1094-2866

Printed in Singapore
First printing 2002

We're here for you!
We at Oxmoor House are dedicated to serving you with reliable information that expands your imagination and enriches your life.

We welcome your comments and suggestions.
Please write us at:
Oxmoor House
Christmas with Country Living
2100 Lakeshore Drive
Birmingham, AL 35209

To order additional publications, call (205) 877-6560 or visit us at www.oxmoorhouse.com

For **COUNTRY LIVING** Magazine
EDITOR IN CHIEF: Nancy Mernit Soriano
DESIGN DIRECTOR: Susan M. Netzel
EXECUTIVE EDITOR: Lawrence A. Bilotti
DEPUTY EDITOR: Marjorie Gage

www.countryliving.com

EDITOR: Bruce Shostak
DESIGNER: Alexis Siroc
Produced by **Smallwood & Stewart, Inc.**, New York City

foreword
8

decorating with **ORNAMENTS**
10

holiday **IN BLOOM**
32

traditional **TARTANS**
60

gilded **WRAPPINGS**
76

Christmas **BREAKFAST**
94

intimate **GATHERING**
104

a sweet sugarplum **FINALE**
124

resources
140

photography credits
143

foreword

Every year, as the holidays approach, our daily lives become a blur of activity: shopping, decorating, entertaining...all while the workaday grind continues as before. And then, all of a sudden, we see the magic of the season in everything around us. From the music in shops to fragrances of the season, from the good wishes of greeting cards to the glitter of ornaments, the signs of good cheer are everywhere. Each day, we see the joy and anticipation in our children's eyes. Before too long the stress has melted away and we realize, all over again, that Christmas is a wonderful time of the year.

At COUNTRY LIVING, we want to make every Christmas more special than the last. We've gathered together wonderful decorating ideas, luscious recipes, and exciting craft projects to inspire you to begin new traditions in your home. We hope that for you and your family this will be a season to remember.

Nancy Mernit Soriano, Editor in Chief

decorating with
ORNAMENTS

They may be vintage, modern, handmade—your favorite baubles and trimmings make decking halls, walls, and windows an annual treat.

A good collection of holiday decorations is years and years in the making. Unlike most other collectibles, Christmas decorations tend to be prized not for their market worth, but by sentimental value. Family heirlooms, gifts from friends, vintage flea-market finds, and luscious new treasures all have special meaning. The richest pieces resonate with memories—the snowflake you made in kindergarten, its glitter still sparkly so many years later, the lopsided paper star your own youngster crafted as a three-year-old. Each precious ornament is lifted from its box with these memories and the promise of a new year of joy.

Glass ornaments are at home just about anywhere. Vintage balls gleam in a milk-glass compote, creating a bouquet that reflects the wintry sun. Urns and ironstone tureens also make elegant display pieces. To complete the look, fresh-cut greens blanket the windowsill and cradle loose balls.

rich vintage
sparkle...

Vintage ornaments are wildly popular. Condition is a factor in their value, but not an overriding one. Tarnish, flaking color, even hairline cracks won't mean an ornament is not presented proudly. It's always a delight to find a hand-painted orb or a set of glass balls in its original box. Missing hooks can be replaced with ribbon, cotton string, or silk cord. After the holiday, store glass ornaments in acid-free paper, in moderate temperature and away from humidity or direct sunlight.

So many country–Christmas lovers are drawn to the nostalgia of vintage decorations. Delicate blown-glass shapes, foil-colored plastic stars, snow-flocked finishes, and finely painted scenics blend harmoniously into the country style. Perhaps because they were for a short season, most ornaments were inexpensive, bought by the dozen in cardboard boxes with cellophane windows. Folks headed over to Woolworth's or Kresge's or some other five-and-ten, or to the local hardware store. Now collectors both passionate and nostalgic scour flea markets, yard sales, local and online auctions, and antique-toy shows to find personal favorites. Manufacturers have geared up to meet the demand, producing reproductions ranging from bubble lights to figural ornaments. Original or reproduction, old-fashioned ornaments bring joy throughout the house.

rich vintage sparkle…

GLITTERING WREATH Antique Christmas balls are dazzling when they're brought together in profusion. To make a holiday wreath (opposite), hot-glue a variety of them to a Styrofoam wreath form. Don't worry if the ornaments have lost their luster—the patina of worn pieces will enhance the wreath's character.

SILVERY SWAG We looped silvery balls on floral wire and tied the cluster to a bough of greenery (right). A cheery polka-dot bow pulls the elements together. Our swag hangs from the handle of a painted tin tray, but it would also look great adorning the frame of a mirror.

KISSING BALL Mistletoe is romantic, but it's not so pretty. Kissing balls, on the other hand, can be beautiful. Make a long-lasting kissing ball with miniature berry red glass ornaments (left). Attach the balls with hot glue to a Styrofoam ball. For best results, make small indentations in the foam with a pencil for the baubles to nestle in. With two large T-pins inserted at different angles, attach a cord for hanging. To finish, hot-glue greenery to the top of the ball and tie ribbon around the cord, into a bow. Clip the edges for a pretty finish.

celebrate
the season with
luster

BEAUTIFUL DREAMERS Even the most ardent advocate of real evergreen trees can be charmed by feather models. Artificial trees fashioned from dyed feathers first became popular in Europe during the late 1800s. By the 1920s, American mail-order houses offered feather trees in a variety of sizes. Many of today's collectors seek out vintage pieces (opposite), but replicas are also available. Whether old or new, feather trees look best when they are sparely dressed. They can comfortably sport a small collection of prized ornaments. For a sweet impression, group a trio of white feather trees (above) on a sofa table, sideboard, or console in the entry hall. Vintage glass birds with nylon bristle tails are the perfectly appropriate toppers.

rich vintage sparkle…

AN ELEGANT EVENT Think beyond the red and green of traditional Christmas. In a light-flooded dining room, a pretty palette of pink, ivory, and soft green looks as if it's stepped out of a fairy-tale. The tree is dressed in shimmery ornaments and swept with graceful strands of silver beads. The evergreen inspires an unusual yet charming and easy tablesetting. Poised on a brilliant white runner, a curvaceous glass urn holds fresh pears and pearlescent ornaments that complement contemporary lusterware. More golden pears are scattered randomly about on the runner. A bundle of fresh thyme tied in sheer ribbon brings fragrance to each place setting. The finishing touch comes in stems of red currants and wisps of pink chiffon swirling from the urn.

Decorating with Ornaments

19

nature's grace...

Most everyone loves a glittery, glowing tree that's heavy with sparkling balls and lights. Still, it's refreshing to turn the clock back to a simpler time. Before folks were able to buy those five-and-ten ornaments, they relied on nature to help trim the tree. Strings of berries were favorite decorations, as were apples and pears, gilded nuts, pinecones, and dried seedpods.

You can still celebrate Christmas with nature. Put the holiday rush on hold and take a hike to gather materials. Spend the afternoon stringing popcorn and peanuts, make pinecones into simple ornaments, or string everything together into a garland. Gild unshelled pecans and walnuts to make glittering trimmings for a miniature evergreen, and glue tiny twigs together to make stars or snowflakes. Finally, trim the windows in your kitchen with fragrant swags of dried fruit slices.

An aromatic kitchen garland (above) features cinnamon sticks and dried apple slices that have been threaded together with raffia. Dried oranges, lemons, limes, and pears also make colorful accents. Homey strands of popcorn, peanuts, and cranberries (opposite) are easy to make with a heavy needle threaded with string or dental floss. For a touch of bright color, add small squares of orange or grapefruit peel to the cranberry garland.

nature's grace…

HOLIDAY FOR THE BIRDS Give back to nature this season by decorating an outside tree for the birds. Deck an evergreen or a bare deciduous tree with pinecones that have been coated in peanut butter and rolled in birdseed. Scatter additional seed, suet, cracked corn, and unsalted peanuts underneath the branches to form a natural tree skirt. Miniature ears of Indian corn delight the birds and bring color to a harsh wintry landscape. To hang the corn, twist a metal screw eye into the end of each ear and then string the screw eyes with jute or cotton cord. Garlands can be hung along a fence or a high hedge; the same ingredients will make a handsome wreath for the front gate. To treat the local squirrels, create a garland of unshelled peanuts.

papers & trims...

For many of us, the first Christmas ornaments we made were paper chains. Regardless of their sophistication or design, paper decorations never go out of style. Earlier generations loved colorful Christmas crafts and transformed bits of paper into scrap-work balls and delicate cornucopias for holiday treats. Creating paper fans was a favorite pastime; ladies made dozens and embellished them with roses, ribbon, and lace. To give this craft a contemporary twist, pleat a selection of pretty papers into graphic circles, or continue making the fans.

To begin your own holiday crafting tradition, save up pieces of paper, ribbon, and gift wrap throughout the year. Look for old Christmas cards at flea markets and tag sales. And don't forget to collect buttons, beads, and fabric remnants. These, too, can be fashioned into decorations with old-fashioned charm.

Pleated and folded bits of paper finished into parasol-like rounds can accent wrapped presents, garlands and trees, or curtain tie-backs. Make a dozen or so and overlap them, like the numerals on a clock, to create a wreath. Keep the look smart by picking colors, patterns, and thicknesses of paper that are harmonious. Like most paper decorations, these are easy to store.

papers & trims...

FUN-TIME TREE Children take the greatest joy in the holidays, so they'd love their own Christmas tree. Set up an evergreen in the playroom (opposite) and enlist the whole family to make decorations from construction paper and playing cards. It's still a *play*room, so stabilize the tree; screw a hook into the ceiling and string fishing line between it and the treetop.

HOLIDAY GREETINGS Vintage calling cards and postcards (right) make enchanting Christmas ornaments. Photocopy favorite images and mount them on sturdy card stock. Punch a hole in the top of each ornament, thread it with satin cord, and slip on glimmering beads.

PAPER DOVES A flock of white doves (left) flutters amid the branches of an airy tree in a down-to-earth galvanized bucket. To create doves, photocopy the template on page 138, enlarging or reducing it as desired. Trace the shape onto paper and cut it out with scissors or a utility knife. Use a hole punch and white ribbon to create the hangers. Strung together doves make a lovely mantel garland; individually, they are terrific gift tags.

every tree deserves
a look
all its own

rag ornaments

Thrifty homemakers have long kept fabric remnants destined for rugs and quilts by shaping them into rag balls. We've taken the tradition a step further by transforming vintage scraps into cheerful country ornaments. Make yours with fabrics on hand or holiday cloths that are too worn for table duty.

Strips of fabric

Styrofoam balls in different sizes

Straight pins

Small felt flowers, homemade or purchased

Tiny beads

Ribbon, trim, or rickrack for hanging

1 Tear or cut the fabric into strips. Choose a starting point on the Styrofoam ball and stick a pin through one strip of fabric. Continue wrapping the ball in fabric strips, sticking pins in to hold them in place, until the ball is completely covered.

2 To add the felt flowers, string pins with tiny beads. Push a pin through the center of each flower into the ball.

3 Attach a loop of ribbon, trim, or rickrack to the top of the ball with two pins inserted at different angles. Hang small rag balls at the top of the tree and larger ones toward the bottom. If you want to make them into hanging window ornaments, alternate the large ones with the small ones.

Poke around in your sewing box for good remnants and buttons.

A little ingenuity transforms them into *glittering snowflakes and elegant garlands,* well within your Christmas budget.

Showy snowflake ornaments (opposite) are simple white or mother-of-pearl buttons and twigs collected from your own backyard. Paint the twigs white; when they're dry, trim them to 7-inch lengths. Hot-glue three twigs together to form a snowflake and allow them to dry. Hot-glue buttons in place. For a pretty window display, attach each ornament to a length of white or silver ribbon and finish with a jingle-bell tassel.

Simple button ornaments take only minutes to make, and kids can easily master them. Thread a large needle with embroidery floss and string a handful of buttons into place. Tie the two ends of the floss together to create a loop, add a ribbon bow, and hang the ornament on a tree.

A garland fashioned from felt and jingle bells (right) brings warmth to a pantry or powder room shelf. Cut felt or felted wool into 1- or 2-inch squares, slightly varying the size of the pieces.

Anchor the garland by threading yarn through a large button. Thread on felt squares, a handful of buttons, a jingle bell, and a few more buttons. Repeat the process until the garland is complete. Add one final button at the end.

holiday
IN BLOOM

With a gentle touch, flowers, fruits, greenery, and bright winter berries remind us that this can be the most gorgeous season of all.

During winter months, we long for the showy splendor of nature's warm weather. Instead, the gardens lie dormant and the landscape fades to a silvery gray. Christmas arrives just in time to lift our spirits. As we craft evergreen garlands and swags, the aromas of the fresh greenery awaken our senses. Bright berries are a flash of vibrant color; citrus fruits refresh the air in stuffy, heated rooms. Perhaps most heartening of all is a humble flowering bulb that has been nurtured into full bloom. We realize that winter can be every bit as breathtaking as spring and summer; there is a difference all right, but this is a difference well worth savoring.

Live flowers are a welcome sight when the weather outside is frightful. Cheer guests—and reward yourself for those endless trips up and down stairs—by lining a wide staircase with cyclamen, amaryllis, and stout vases of fresh-cut flowers. For a touch of green, slip a few topiaries into the mix.

crimson & snow...

Decorating with red for the holidays is a natural. After all, red is one of the most festive colors ever devised by Mother Nature. Just picture the holly branch, its shiny green leaves edged in white, its stems laden with vivid berries. When paired with white, red is shown to its radiant advantage. There's nothing quite as pretty as a bouquet of rich crimson tulips in a snowy urn or a deep red pepperberry wreath on a white-washed door.

As you prepare for the Christmas season, look for simple ways to bring touches of red and white to your home. Scour cupboards for milk glass, ironstone, and plain white china. These materials all make wonderful backdrops for showcasing the brilliance of flowers, fruits, and berries. Fill a compote with a copious amount of fresh cranberries, pile red apples into a topiary atop a cake stand, or float miniature roses in bowls.

A white demitasse cup (above) holds a single, full-blown red ranunculus and two variegated holly leaves. Position miniature bouquets at place settings for a dinner party or group them in bunches to bring color to the dessert table. Your favorite collections need not go into hiding for the holidays. White painted baskets (opposite) mix beautifully with canola berries, cranberries, and shiny apples.

crimson & snow...

HOLIDAY DINNER Splash the dining room with color for Christmas. Slipcover chairs with a bright floral pattern (opposite) and crown the table with an arrangement of fresh tulips. Windows and walls wear wreaths and swags of contrasting green.

AT FIRESIDE In a white room, a little red will go a long way. Decorate the mantel with a single rope of cranberries (right). The vivid red of amaryllis, tulips, and miniature roses is underplayed by a collection of white pottery. Paper-whites continue the botanical theme without stealing the show.

YOU'RE WELCOME For a memorable party favor, wrap small gifts in white paper tied with snowy chiffon ribbon. Place one in a cranberry-glass compote for each guest (below). Crisp white linens and crystal bring enchantment to the table.

let nature bring a
burst
of color

In chilly December, the most thoughtful Christmas present is a gift from nature. It doesn't take an expert gardener to coax *beautiful, fragrant flowers from dormant bulbs.*

For years, flowering branches have been brought indoors and forced to bloom for the holidays—forsythia, cherry blossoms, and quince are popular examples. Flowering bulbs can be fooled into believing that spring is on its way by storing them for several weeks in the refrigerator. Once they're potted, set in room temperatures, and bathed in daylight, they begin the blooming process. A single bulb in its own pot makes a longer-lasting gift (left). Make them a bit more glamorous by wrapping colorful ribbon around the pots.

Paper-whites, the narcissus bulbs that look like miniature daffodils, do not need to be precooled, and are among the most eager to bring out their delicate flowers. To ready them for friends (opposite), bind the stems with fluffy white yarn and adorn the pots with sleeves cut from old ski sweaters. Cover the soil with a decorative layer of sphagnum moss and pinecones.

Begin forcing paper-whites about a month before you want them to bloom. Fill a shallow watertight container with pebbles or gravel to roughly an inch below the top. Bury the bulbs an inch apart with the tops exposed. Pour in just enough water to reach the bottoms of the bulbs and place them in a cool spot. Keep the water level constant. As roots and shoots emerge, move the plants to a warmer room.

FIR POMANDERS In place of a single kissing ball, display a chorus of lush fir pomanders (opposite). Wrap supple sprigs around Styrofoam balls and secure them with U-shape floral greening pins. Wrap each ball in bright gingham ribbon and tie several bows at the top. These look fine on a hall table, in a basket or an urn.

A WINTER PICNIC When flowers are hard to come by, create inventive bouquets from simple things found around the house. A case in point: For a casual holiday buffet, group red-handled Bakelite flatware in a tin bucket (left). Slip in a sprig of spruce with a snip of plaid ribbon and head for the table.

CANDY CANES The milkman may not come along every morning, but his old glass bottles are still coveted. Recycle quart milk bottles and pint cream bottles by turning them into holders for candy canes (right). If you're lucky enough to have one, group them in a wire bottle holder from the dairy. You've created a centerpiece that is old-fashioned, fragrant, and delicious.

unexpected
touches
bring some
whimsy

a festival of fruits...

Fruits have long been the jewels of winter. For earlier generations, the aroma of freshly peeled oranges or tangerines in many homes meant only one thing—the holidays had arrived. Citrus fruits were so precious that they were lovingly tucked into stockings as a treat for Christmas morning. Winter fruits still hold a special place on cold weather tables. Vibrant lemons, limes, kumquats, and clementines adapt to formal and impromptu centerpieces. When their peel is studded with cloves, citrus fruits are even more aromatic and decorative.

Look to apples and cranberries for traditional touches of red. As an elegant presentation, set your holiday dessert buffet with a pedestal stand of sugared fruits. Even more dramatic is a trio of stands, each tier laden with sugary grapes, cherries, figs, and lady apples. Fill out the arrangement with glass balls.

A gilded pear filled with fresh roses (above) is a lovely grace note for the table. To make the miniature centerpiece, cover a pear with gold floral spray. Slice the top from the fruit and hollow out the bottom with a melon baller. Pour in water and insert flowers, berries, and greens. For an easy, quick splash of color at an informal meal (opposite), line the table with vintage mixing bowls of oranges, apples, and lemons.

a festival of fruits…

ELEGANT SIDEBOARD To dress up the dining room, showcase towers of fruit on the sideboard. The spot offers the advantage of being away from the table, so that the decoration will not interfere with conversation and interrupt passing platters. Groups of three always look best, and be sure to vary the height of the arrangements. A display of fruit can be more interesting if it is filled out with fresh flowers. For the dessert course, we've layered pears, kumquats, roses, and grapes on a tower of handsome glass cake stands. The rich palette of the fruit complements the mulberryware on the wall. To complete the scene, smaller arrangements of roses and pears appear along the length of the table.

being
original...

Once upon a time, centerpieces were required to be proper and predictable. A hostess wouldn't dream of setting a table with anything but her best china and a centerpiece designed to command everyone's full attention.

Now, holiday dinners are elegant or casual, but the rules are relaxed. Humble natural ornaments often take center stage, and we enjoy decorating with sentimental items from our own collections. A centerpiece can be created from just about anything that strikes fancy—a rustic wood dough bowl, an elegant urn, even a garden statue.

Be fearless when you mix traditional and whimsical elements. Set amaryllis in a glass beaker filled with colorful cranberries or marbles. Arrange white roses in a galvanized pail. Hang children's woolen mittens on an evergreen.

A fanciful birdcage (above) joins the festivities when it is decked with a wreath of shiny leaves and a trio of mercury glass balls. An old tin vessel (opposite) echoes the simplicity of the tin stars and snowflakes hung on its miniature tree. Some small evergreens bought from a nursery can be taken outside when the holidays wind down, depending on how long they've been indoors.

being original…

REFLECTED GLORY Three pillar candles (opposite) assume a glowing presence in front of a large overmantel mirror. Wrap them in wide ribbon and glue pepperberries in place. Tie a narrow ribbon around each candle as a finishing touch.

SWEET CENTERPIECE Bright red amaryllis (right) rise from a sea of sweet peppermint pillows. Place a tumbler or vase in a hurricane on a large plate and cover it with plastic wrap. Pour the candy around the tumbler until it reaches the top of the glass. Remove the plastic wrap, fill the tumbler with water, and slip in trimmed amaryllis stems.

FAVORITE FINDS Combine cherished collections and flea-market bounty (below) for interesting holiday displays. Sparkling mercury glass and vintage baubles offset the rustic appeal of a homespun snowman.

the freshest displays
are surprisingly
simple

ON THE WATERFRONT Sort through your own collections for clever containers. We've taken a rustic model canoe (above) and filled it to the brim with fragrant eucalyptus and berries. Protect metal or wood containers by lining them with heavy plastic before filling them with greens. If a container isn't watertight, keep the flowers fresh in floral vials.

NATURAL WARMTH A treetop in a garden bucket (opposite) doesn't require any trimming at all when it is surrounded by tea lights that glow merrily from canning jars. Potted plants and boxwood topiaries complete the holiday vignette. Recruited from an antique dollhouse, loopy picket fencing surrounds the plants to create the feeling of a country garden.

classical

urns...

So many people think of urns as items that belong in the garden. In fact, outdoor urns can be made of cast iron or concrete, as well as lightweight and less expensive fiberglass. During the winter months these can be planted with small conifers or simply left alone to become icy sculptures when cold weather sets in. A matching pair looks handsome when it has been fitted with a topiary of holiday greens and enlisted to stand sentry at a doorway.

But urns are just as beautiful indoors, especially when they appear in unexpected ways. Dress smaller urns with fresh fruit, sparkling glass ornaments, or a white amaryllis in bloom. A large sturdy urn can support the Christmas tree itself. And urns can be filled with presents, firewood, glass ornaments—whatever comes to hand.

A traditional apple topiary (above) is lifted to elegant heights in a cast-iron urn. Snips of boxwood cradle the glowing candle at top. The apples are arranged on a nail-studded wooden form that dates back to Colonial times. Gazing balls set within tall stone urns (opposite) heighten the drama at the fireplace. Finish the arrangements with pine branches.

classical urns...

WHITE CHRISTMAS A graceful iron urn with distressed white paint (opposite) holds a delicate amaryllis that has been forced from a bulb—a perfect symbol of the old giving birth to the new.

A LIGHT IN WINTER Urns can function as well as decorate. Candle-filled urns (right) can light a walkway leading to a party or form a group on an outside terrace. For variety, choose pinecones for some urns and silver balls for others; natural pinecones, sparkling glass, and glowing candles create unexpected harmony.

SNOWBALL SCULPTURE Garden urns needn't be neglected during the winter months. What could be as simple and yet as elegant as a graceful pyramid of perfect snowballs on a bed of evergreens and berries (below): It's a festive showpiece.

a white urn
echoes the
beauty
of winter

outdoor
spirit...

The best holiday decorations blend with the surrounding architecture. A stone house (opposite) takes on an almost magical aura when lit by candles on a rough-hewn table. The rustic front door (above) boasts a holly wreath accented with a pair of old hockey skates and thick wool skating socks.

Deep in December, a home is not just a place to live. It is a refuge from wintry blasts and offers a cheerful light during the long winter nights. Family, friends, and neighbors drop by to escape the cold while caroling or to extend holiday greetings. Nothing could be more inviting to guests than a walkway lined with luminaries—paper bags filled partly with sand and lighted from the inside with glowing candles. Lanterns hung from the limbs of a barren tree will create a luminous display against a backdrop of freshly fallen snow.

Outdoor decor is most effective when it echoes the style of the house. An elegant Georgian can support a profusion of lush evergreens, but a seaside cottage looks just right with a single seashell wreath on the door. Wreaths made from prickly pears or chili peppers reflect the spirit of the Southwest.

A STAR IS HUNG Don't be afraid to break with tradition. A weathered metal star (left) is just as festive as an evergreen wreath, and it sets one doorway apart from the rest. Two stone roosters, standing guard at the entrance, wear the wreaths.

SEASONAL SYMMETRY A wreath calls attention to any door, but its job is made easier if it is properly framed. A slightly oval evergreen wreath (opposite) echoes the shape of the ornate screen door. Tall arrangements of decorative twigs on either side of the entrance suggest a second frame.

HOLIDAY HOLDERS A red sap bucket filled with boxwood (right) extends a unique Christmas greeting on a plain paneled door. Sap buckets are natural choices, as they were designed with holes near the top for hanging from tree trunks. A bit of ribbon makes it all jolly.

deck your
front door with
style

traditional
TARTANS

Plaids may invoke romantic images of heather, kilts, and bagpipes, but they are evocative, as well, of Christmas, especially in red and green.

Tartan plaids are the essence of old-fashioned Christmas. With their rich colors and lush woolen weaves, they bring reassuring comfort; it's hardly possible to look at them and not hear frosty jingle bells. Tartan-inspired ribbons and wrapping papers dress gifts; tartanware boxes and picture frames are wonderful presents. While a log cabin or stone farmhouse is the ideal backdrop for tartan decorations, the plaids fit seamlessly into any environment. If you live in a city apartment, just wrap your wreath in wide tartan taffeta. Does your taste run to the spare country look? A lone tartan throw will bring the mood of the holiday to any piece of furniture.

Tartan patterns on boxes, frames, and a match caddy inspire a mantel that serves its stone surroundings well. Create the same effect by wrapping boxes and other decorative items with scraps of fabric or paper. To finish the look, choose a complementary ribbon for the wreath.

highland
legacy...

In 1850 Prince Albert bought Balmoral Palace for Queen Victoria and Scotland became a fashionable destination for English holiday-seekers. The new surge in tourism meant popularity for the country's many family tartans, and it brought about the creation of souvenirs of tartan-patterned fabrics—especially those outstanding wools—as well as,

For a thoughtful house gift (above), slip red candles into a silver julep cup. Dress an ordinary matchbox in a tartan sleeve; just glue on a bit of ribbon that is the same width as the matchbox. A room with a fireplace (opposite) becomes even cozier when plaids have arrived. Drape a tree with bright red ribbon and, with shorter strands, tie bundles of cinnamon sticks to the branches.

tartans on napkin rings, sewing items, and notions. More than a century later, tartanware objects are even more highly collectible, and plaids continue to have a place in our homes, particularly in winter. As the temperature drops, that tartan muffler promises relief from the cold; those tartan blankets beckon us to cuddle up. It's little wonder, then, that tartan is such a successful holiday decorating motif; it's seasonal, cheery, beautiful, and comforting, all at once.

THE PAPER CHASE If you're dreaming of a plaid Christmas, create a supply of gift-wrapping goods with interesting papers and a selection of complementary ribbons in reds, blues, and greens. A few rolls of brown kraft paper or white freezer paper will play along handsomely with the rich colors of the tartan. Plaid fabric remnants also make stylish wraps.

TARTAN CARTON A plain cardboard box becomes a festive container for short-bread cookies or peanut brittle when it's covered in a colorful plaid. Wrap the lid in a solid color and attach ball fringe with hot glue. Add a final layer of red ribbon to conceal the top of the fringe. For a keep-sake piece, choose a sturdy wood or metal box and wrap it in durable wallpaper.

Classic tartans make *festive gifts for your faithful companion* and the animal lovers on your list.

Dogs and cats look bonnie in plaid during the holidays.

Black and white photographs (opposite top) become adorable hanging ornaments that look their best surrounded by bright tartan. You can make the frames with thin cardboard and one-inch-wide plaid ribbon. Measure the photo and add an inch on each side for ribbon. Double the dimensions to form a front and back for the frame, and cut it out of cardboard. Fold the cardboard in half, unfold it, and cut an opening on one side for the picture. Cut pieces of ribbon for the frame, miter the edges, and glue them in place. Conceal the seams on each corner with thin velvet ribbon. Insert the photo and a satin ribbon for hanging before gluing the frame shut.

Just like Chester the pug, every pet deserves a smart dress collar for holiday soirées (opposite bottom). Top-stitch plaid ribbon to a length of felt that has been cut with pinking shears. Attach Velcro at the ends to make a fastener, and stitch on a wooden dog bone or a jingle bell. When your pet is poised upon his own tartan pillow, the look is complete.

Avoid confusion under the tree, and wrap your dog's gift in a package fit for a pooch (left). With a rubber stamp and black ink, make paw prints on a bare box or plain white paper. The finishing touch? A tartan ribbon paired with playful Scottie trim.

fabric

crafts...

It only seems natural to include plaid fabrics to your holiday mix, but you're not limited to fine Highlander wools. Recycle bits and pieces like old flannel shirts, pajamas, and winter scarves that have seen better days. When it is altered into a tree trimming or a holiday craft, a favorite article of clothing will give many more seasons of pleasure.

A warm palette of browns and golds creates a gentle Christmas scene. Cocoa-color pom-pom garlands circle the tree, while taffeta bows and golden glass balls bring extra elegance. A favorite patchwork skirt has been recycled into crazy-quilt partridges for the tree. The tails are made from peacock plumes.

Fabric scraps of all types can be stitched together for patchwork ornaments, stocking trims, and Christmas tree skirts. In lieu of customary plaid ribbons, tie strips of tartan taffeta to the tree to form bows. To prevent fraying, trim the fabric with pinking shears. Select a tartan palette that echoes the colors already in your rooms. Feel free to eschew red and green. Instead you might choose muted plaids in warm earth tones or soft pastels. and combine them with touches of gold.

plaid wreath

You can enjoy hanging this plaid wreath year after year. Spruce it up with fresh greenery and berries when the holidays arrive.

Red velvet fabric

One 16-inch foam or straw wreath form

1/2 yard each of 3 different plaid fabrics

2 yards red ribbon 2-inches wide for bow

Red grosgrain ribbon 3-inches wide for hanging

T-pins

Variegated ivy and pepperberry sprigs

Scissors

Glue gun

1 Cut the velvet into strips 8" wide and 6" long. Turn under the cut edges and seal with hot glue.

2 Wrap velvet strips around the wreath and secure on back with straight pins. The fabric should be flat and completely cover the wreath.

3 Cut the plaid fabrics into strips 10" wide and 8" long. You'll need 3 strips of one plaid fabric and 2 strips each of the other two patterns. Finish the edges as in Step #1.

4 Loosely wrap the plaid strips around the wreath form, securing it on the back with T-pins. Alternate the patterns for the best effect.

5 Garnish the wreath with variegated ivy and pepperberry sprigs. Tie red ribbon into a bow and secure it with hot glue. Glue a length of ribbon for hanging to the top.

ruffled stocking

Even a beginner can sew some tartan stockings. These aren't just for plaids, though; make them up in whatever crazy combinations you like. For a ruffled stocking, enlarge the template on page 139.

1/4 to 1/2 yard wool

24" solid-color satin ribbon, 1/2"-wide

1 1/2 yards 4" wide plaid cotton fabric

Straight pins

Fabric marker or chalk for tracing

Sewing machine with ruffler attachment

Ribbon for hanging

1 Fold the fabric in half with right sides facing, and pin the template to it. Trace the template onto the fabric, leaving an additional 1/2" around the stocking. Cut through both layers of fabric to create the front and back of the stocking.

2 Pin the front and back together with right sides of fabric facing. Sew the pieces of fabric together, stopping 2 1/2" below the top of stocking at the back. Do not sew across the opening of the stocking. Turn stocking right side out.

3 To create the ruffle, turn under one edge of the plaid cotton fabric and stitch to finish. Use the ruffler attachment on a sewing machine to ruffle the fabric.

4 Fold over the top 1/4" edge of the stocking to form a small cuff and press with an iron. Pin the top edge of the ribbon to the top of the cuff, starting at the opening in back. Sew the top edge of the ribbon in place. Pin the ruffle and the bottom edge of the ribbon to the stocking, making sure that the ruffle hangs nicely. Sew in place.

5 Turn the stocking inside out and sew up the final 2" of stocking. Sew a loop of ribbon inside the stocking to form a hanger.

plaid stocking

Want a good decoration for the guest room? Stitch up a plaid stocking and fill it with a puzzle book, a scented candle, guest soaps, and a candy cane. Hang it from the doorknob and you've said Welcome!

1/4 to 1/2 yard plaid fabric

24" solid color ribbon, 1" or wider

4" square of wool for heel

Straight pins

Fabric marker or chalk for tracing

Ribbon for hanging

1 Enlarge the template on page 139 and cut it out. Fold the plaid fabric in half with right sides facing, and pin the template to it. Trace the template onto the fabric, leaving an additional 1/2" all the way around the stocking. Cut through both layers of fabric.

2 Enlarge the heel template on page 139 and cut it out. Fold the wool in half with right sides facing each other, and pin the template to it. Trace the template onto fabric, leaving an additional 1/2" all the way around the heel. Cut through both layers of fabric. Sew the heels onto the front and back of the stocking.

3 Pin the front and back stocking pieces together with right sides facing. Sew the two pieces of fabric together, stopping 2 1/2" below the top of stocking at the back. Do not sew across the opening of the stocking. Turn the stocking right side out.

4 Fold over the top 1/4" edge of the stocking to form a small cuff and press with an iron. Pin the ribbon to the cuff, starting at the opening in back. Sew the ribbon in place at the top and bottom.

5 Turn the stocking inside out and sew up the top 2" of stocking. Sew a loop of ribbon inside the stocking to form a hanger.

gilded
WRAPPINGS

With a little ingenuity, you can turn any package into a work of art. Once you get the hang of it, you will invent easy, personal ways to wrap.

The elegantly wrapped Christmas gift is as American as apple pie. For many years, holiday gifts weren't wrapped at all—they were nestled within the boughs of the evergreen tree or piled beneath the branches. Gift wrap became popular during the 1870s and 1880s, but packages then were simply dressed, perhaps with white tissue paper and a sprig of holly. That is, until the Hall Brothers in Missouri (yes, they became the Hallmark company) began selling fancy papers. Now the presentation is part and parcel of gift-giving. The wrap can be inspired by the present within, or by the recipient, or by the giver, so long as it heightens the anticipation.

If you have a bibliophile on your list, cover packages in pages photocopied from vintage books. Choose from the works of a favorite author or select an excerpt from a Christmas classic like *The Gift of the Magi*. Sheet music and pages from old magazines also make cheerful, graphic wraps.

ribbons & trims...

To turn pretty ribbons into gift tags (above), all you need is a steady hand and an indelible marker with metallic ink. Rubber alphabet stamps can personalize gifts too. A stack of Christmas presents (opposite) becomes even more fetching when it bears a message insisting the recipient wait until Christmas.

When it comes to wrapping gifts, we are spoiled for choice. Specialty papers, some even handmade, are available locally and by mail, as are ribbons and fabrics from around the world. But imagination, not expense, is the driving force of beautiful, clever, enticing gift wraps. Newspapers like the Sunday comics or foreign language editions, photographs copied onto white paper, and fabrics like felt or organdy can be wrapped around a gift, then topped with ribbons of organdy, satin, silk velvet, and grosgrain. White or red cotton kitchen string can replace ribbon; so can raffia. A big beautiful bow may be the finish, or the package might be adorned with jewelry, buttons, silk flowers, tiny trucks, toy soldiers, papier-mâché cherries, miniature wood blocks, whatever catches your fancy. The final element? A distinctive tag.

SPECIAL FAVORS Small details make the difference. A group of party favors becomes a beguiling centerpiece (opposite) when the gifts are tied with silver tinsel and displayed in a milk-glass compote. Clusters of artificial berries complement the icy tones. An old quilt or chenille spread can be cut to make fabric garlands and candy canes.

FASHION STATEMENT When the box itself is beautiful, focus your energy on creating one-of-a-kind trims. Sewing shops and millinery supply stores offer a variety of flourishes. We combined beaded fruit with silky moiré ribbon (right) to make a gift of soaps even more luxurious.

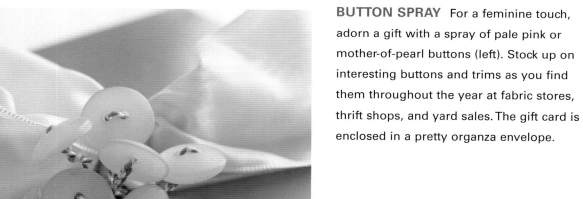

BUTTON SPRAY For a feminine touch, adorn a gift with a spray of pale pink or mother-of-pearl buttons (left). Stock up on interesting buttons and trims as you find them throughout the year at fabric stores, thrift shops, and yard sales. The gift card is enclosed in a pretty organza envelope.

adorn
a gift with dressmaker details

Express your thoughtfulness and creativity with a *homemade gift tag* personalized especially for the recipient. It becomes as enjoyable as the present itself.

Elegant ribbons seem even more beautiful when they're paired with plain papers and natural materials (opposite center). Showcase a filigree ribbon against white paper or mix silky trimmings with nubby pinecones.

Even autumn leaves enliven Christmas gifts. Gather leaves in the fall, press them, and stash them away until the holidays arrive. To make a gift tag (opposite above right), cut the leaf shape from card stock and translucent art paper. Mount the leaf to the card stock, cover with the overlay, and make a hole for the ribbon.

Baby pinecones, fresh greens, and winter berries bring natural color to holiday parcels. For a present that's going to be given right away, create a gift tag by threading silver cord through fresh holly leaves (opposite below left). Tie on a sprig of juniper berries and personalize the tag with a message written in indelible ink.

For an environmentally-friendly gift, decorate a package with a gift tag that contains seeds for post-holiday planting (below), cut in a tree shape from paper that has been embedded with seeds. The papers are available at garden centers; choose seeds for a plant that grows well in the recipient's area.

specialty
papers...

Few items can be as intriguing as a gift that's been wrapped and decorated by hand. Create your own wrapping paper designs and your presents will stand out from all the others.

Before the holiday rush begins, devote an afternoon to making gift wrap with your family or with a circle of friends. Prepare for the day by stocking up on brown kraft paper, white butcher's paper, and plain wrapping papers in red and green. Other supplies will depend on the project. Papers can be painted freehand, embellished with stencils, or sponged with metallic paint. Purchase rubber stamps, or make your own stamp designs from raw potatoes to apply acrylic paint. But homespun papers don't have to be painstakingly crafted for pretty results. Extraordinary packages can be created with simple stickers and stationery supplies.

Coordinating wraps and cards (above) complement each other; gold and silver stamp pads produce dazzling results. For a lively contrast, decorate red wrapping paper with white acrylic paint (opposite). We worked with a checkerboard stamp to create this design, but other motifs would be just as striking. The goal is not to achieve something perfect, but something personal.

POLKA DOTS Ordinary stickers from the office-supply store (left) are reinvented into festive polka dots when applied to holiday packages. The dots bring such a lively energy to plain papers.

FORGET THE BOX Make gift bags to just the size you need for oddly shaped presents (opposite). Enlarge and cut out the template on page 138. Fold it into a bag shape, unfold it, and tack it to the underside of the wrapping paper with tape. Cut the paper and fold the paper as indicated into a bag. Remove the template, refold the bag, and glue the bottom.

SNOW FLURRIES Pinking shears and a snowflake punch are all you need to turn strips of paper into fanciful ribbon (below). Don't let the white snowflakes go to waste. Glue them to any package to create the look of fluffy snowflakes.

even stationery
supplies can be
festive

by golly, jolly wraps...

One of the most satisfying ways to jazz up the Christmas scene is to jazz up your palette. Turn your gift-wrap station on its ear with a rainbow of deep cobalt, sienna, purple, and yellow. Or consider wrapping packages in rich jewel tones like ruby, topaz, citrine. Then again, be inspired by the gourmet produce that's so prevalent now: Concord grapes, figs, clementines, chestnuts.

Vintage fabrics and trims often have exquisite colors. When you visit flea markets and antiques shows, keep an eye out for luxury velvets, silks, and brocades; look at homey cotton chenilles, tickings, and floral prints. The tassels on a tattered curtain and the silk flowers from an old hat are such exquisite decorations, and you need so little that even small scraps are put to good use. Toss convention to the wind and be bold pairing these elements; you'll seldom have more fun.

Sumptuous stockings in rich fabrics and passementerie (opposite) are sure to be hung from the chimney year after year. Odd bits of vintage milliners' supplies and notions were conceived as trimmings, making them natural ornaments. A festive fruit bouquet (above) was fashioned from vintage, new, and recycled finds. Any gorgeous stocking deserves to conceal within at least one super-special present.

PRETTY IN PINK Deck your walls in shades of pale and hot pink. The color is dazzling at Christmas (opposite) and it will still look seasonal come Valentine's Day. Parcels wrapped, bound with bright ribbons, and stacked in a chair become a decoration in themselves.

GIFT BOX The most memorable part of a gift can be the box itself. A handcrafted candy basket (right) would be proudly displayed atop any girl's dresser. Small presents can also be tucked inside a new purse or evening bag.

RETRO WRAP We've souped up a baby gift with polka dots and bright fuchsia ribbon (below), but the wrap would be equally suitable for a teenager or young adult. A beaded keepsake gift tag reinforces the retro look.

bring zip to
the holiday—think
pink

Whether you've collected them over time or just run out to the

crafts store, *glittery notions and gems* take packages

from ordinary to fantastic.

Regal trims don't have to cost a king's ransom. Inexpensive plastic jewels can be found at most crafts stores. A variety of colors and shapes will embellish ribbons and gift tags alike.

A store's notions department is often a treasure of colorful cords and braids. Bargain-priced remnants are too good to pass up. Personalize a gift by shaping jewel-toned strands of sequins into elegant initials (opposite). A metallic buckle can dress up the ribbon on a holiday package.

For a teacher, a coach, or the world's greatest dad, award a first-prize ribbon (left). Cut one circle from red paper with pinking shears and a slightly smaller circle of coordinating paper with regular scissors. Cut two widths of ribbon to the desired length. Glue the circles together, add the ribbon at the bottom, and inscribe the tag with the name or a special message. Glue on jewels.

Have lustrous goods at hand when you need them; stock up on iridescent ribbons, silky tassels, and small metallic baubles. For sparkle without the color, adorn packages with rhinestones, pearls, crystal beads, or creamy white sequins.

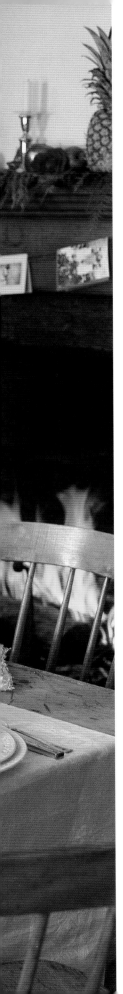

Christmas
BREAKFAST

It's the best morning of the year. Generous and comforting food, everyone gathered around the table: This is a glorious way to celebrate.

Who doesn't love Christmas dinner? But if you think about it, breakfast can be the most celebratory meal of the season. As the house comes alive on Christmas morning, spirits are high and children race for the tree. Everyone is together, ready for the long-awaited merriment. His long journey finished, Santa's having a good cup of coffee; now's the time to brew up a pot for your gang. Fill some mugs with hot chocolate, cut up some fresh fruit, and tear into those gifts. Later, settle in for a lazy meal and relive the excitement of the morning. Feel the holiday pace soften, as you unwind and enjoy the real magic of Christmas.

Let your table become a stage for the joy and warmth of Christmas morning. Consider setting it up right next to the fireplace or the Christmas tree. Bring out those heirlooms as serving pieces, and create a simple centerpiece just by piling fresh fruit atop a cake stand. Greet sleepy diners with a blazing fire.

a family affair...

Continue the morning's revelry by letting everyone open one final gift at the breakfast table. Tiny packages topped with gingerbread men will please children and adults alike. At a buffet, folks relax with their plates. If you order a spiral-sliced ham, you won't need to spend time carving.

Our hearty Christmas breakfast features a medley of longtime family favorites—a smoked ham, home fries, and a winter fruit compote with apricots, kumquats, and cranberries. Children will delight in helping to make a show-stopping Christmas tree with frozen dough, and no one—absolutely no one—will resist chocolate crêpes with banana-cream.

Above all else, breakfast should be relaxing. You don't want to toil away in the kitchen, away from family eager for your company, so many of these recipes can be prepared completely, or at least partially, ahead of time. The precooked ham does need to be heated up in the oven, but its savory glaze can be made even one week ahead. The cider can be simmered on Christmas Eve and quickly reheated in the morning, as everyone heads for the table.

vegetable strata

SAVORY SIDE DISH Vegetable strata is quickly assembled the day before and popped in the oven on Christmas morning. The Mediterranean-inspired recipe blends tomatoes, spinach, and sautéed fennel with Asiago and provolone cheeses. It makes an interesting side dish for breakfast or brunch, but it can also serve as a supper entrée during the holiday week.

SWEET & SIMPLE Crêpes may seem intimidating for Christmas morning, but they can actually be made two weeks in advance, wrapped tightly in plastic, and frozen. Make the banana-cream filling the day before and chill it in the refrigerator. On Christmas morning simply warm the crêpes for a few seconds in the microwave, add the filling, and roll them up.

banana-cream crêpes

with raspberry sauce

spiral-sliced smoked ham

Makes 16 servings

What meat can glide so smoothly from hearty breakfast to tasty lunch to elegant dinner and even to a satisfying supper? Your family will adore this.

One 20-ounce can crushed unsweetened pineapple with juice

1/2 cup firmly packed light brown sugar

1 tablespoon butter

1/8 teaspoon ground cloves

1/3 cup dried cherries

One 5- to 6-pound spiral-sliced smoked ham

1. **make glaze** In the bowl of a food processor fitted with a chopping blade, blend the pineapple with juice, the brown sugar, the butter, and the cloves until puréed. Transfer the mixture to a 2-quart saucepan and bring it to a boil over high heat. Reduce the heat to medium and cook, stirring occasionally, until the mixture thickens, 20 to 25 minutes. Remove the glaze from the heat and stir in the dried cherries.

2. **cook ham** Preheat the oven to 350°F. Place the ham in a large roasting pan. Brush the glaze over the ham and cook until the ham has warmed through, 30 to 45 minutes. Serve warm.

golden home fries

Makes 8 servings

Here is the only hands-on dish we think meets the standards of Christmas breakfast.

2 pounds Yukon Gold potatoes, peeled and cut into 1/2-inch cubes

3/4 teaspoon salt, plus more for cooking water

2 pounds sweet potatoes, peeled and cut into 1/2-inch cubes

3 tablespoons butter

1 large onion, coarsely chopped

2 cloves garlic, finely chopped

1/2 teaspoon ground black pepper

1. **prepare potatoes** Place the Yukon Gold potatoes in a 4-quart saucepan and cover with salted water by 3 inches. Bring to a boil over high heat; cook 2 minutes. Carefully add the sweet potatoes and return to a boil. Cook until the potatoes are fork tender and still firm, 10 to 12 minutes. Drain and place the potatoes on a large baking sheet in a single layer to cool.

2. **combine ingredients** In a large heavy skillet, melt the butter over medium heat. Add the onion and cook until softened and translucent, 5 to 7 minutes. Add the garlic and cook 1 minute more. Add the potatoes, 3/4 teaspoon salt, and the black pepper to the skillet. Cook, stirring occasionally, until the potatoes are crispy browned and cooked through, 15 to 20 minutes. Serve immediately.

vegetable strata

Makes 12 servings

An abundance of Italian Asiago and provolone cheeses, milk, and eggs, combine with vegetables—fennel, tomatoes, and spinach—to bake up into a delicious casserole.

3 tablespoons olive oil

1 medium fennel bulb, trimmed and chopped

1 medium onion, thinly sliced

3 cloves garlic, sliced

One 14 1/2-ounce can diced tomatoes

1 tablespoon Dijon-style mustard

8 cups coarsely chopped spinach

1/4 teaspoon ground black pepper

1/4 teaspoon dried oregano leaves

1/4 teaspoon salt

12 slices firm white bread, crusts removed

1/3 pound shredded Asiago cheese

1/3 pound shredded provolone cheese

3 cups milk

6 large eggs

1. **sauté vegetables** Grease a 9- by 13-inch baking dish. In a large skillet, heat the olive oil over medium heat. Add the fennel and sauté 10 minutes. Add the onion and sauté until the vegetables have lightly browned, 8 to 10 minutes. Add the garlic and cook 1 minute more. Stir in the tomatoes and mustard; cook until the tomatoes soften, 10 to 12 minutes. Stir in the spinach, pepper, oregano, and salt; cook 1 minute more. Remove the skillet from the heat and let cool 10 minutes.

2. **layer strata** Arrange half the bread in the bottom of the prepared baking dish. Top with half of the vegetable mixture, half the Asiago cheese, and half the provolone cheese. Repeat the layering with the remaining bread, the vegetables, and the cheeses.

3. In a large bowl, lightly beat together the milk and eggs; pour over the vegetable-and-cheese mixture.

4. **bake casserole** Preheat the oven to 350°F. Cook the strata, uncovered, until the center appears set, 40 to 50 minutes. Serve immediately.

winter-fruit compote

Makes 12 servings

This elegant compote is to canned fruit cocktail what fresh tuna is to canned—a supreme improvement.

2 cups white grape juice

3/4 cup sugar

Two 3-inch cinnamon sticks

1 star anise

4 whole cloves

3 medium-firm pears, peeled and quartered

1 cup dried apricots, cut in half

1 cup prunes

1/2 cup dried cranberries

6 kumquats, cut horizontally into 1/4-inch slices

1 large navel orange, peeled and sectioned

1. **combine ingredients** In a saucepan, combine the grape juice, 1 cup water, the sugar, cinnamon sticks, star anise, and cloves. Bring to a boil over medium heat. Reduce the heat to low; add the pears, apricots, prunes, and cranberries. Cover and simmer to soften the fruit, 15 to 20 minutes.

2. **serve compote** Stir in the kumquats. Remove the pan from the heat and let cool 15 minutes. Remove and discard the star anise and cloves. Stir in the orange segments and serve.

banana-cream crêpes with raspberry sauce

Makes 2 dozen

It's Christmas morning, and there is no better time to pamper your family with a fabulous dessert at breakfast. Make crêpes in chocolate and vanilla flavors, just because it's fun to have both.

chocolate crêpes

1 cup unsifted all-purpose flour

1/2 cup Dutch-processed cocoa powder

1/2 cup confectioners' sugar

1/4 teaspoon salt

4 large eggs

2 1/2 cups milk

3 tablespoons vegetable oil

1 teaspoon pure vanilla extract

vanilla crêpes

1 3/4 cups unsifted all-purpose flour

1/4 cup confectioners' sugar

1/4 teaspoon salt

4 large eggs

2 1/2 cups milk

3 tablespoons vegetable oil

1 teaspoon pure vanilla extract

Vegetable-oil cooking spray, for crêpe pan

raspberry sauce

2 cups fresh or frozen red raspberries

1/3 cup granulated sugar

2 tablespoons brandy (optional)

banana-cream filling

2 cups heavy cream

One 3-ounce package cream cheese, softened

1/4 cup confectioners' sugar

6 very ripe bananas, mashed

1/4 teaspoon ground cinnamon

1. **prepare chocolate crêpes** In a medium bowl, combine the flour, the cocoa powder, the confectioners' sugar, and the salt. In another bowl, with a wire whisk, beat the eggs, milk, oil, and vanilla until smooth. Let the mixture stand 5 minutes to thicken.

2. **prepare vanilla crêpes** In a medium bowl, combine the flour, confectioners' sugar, and salt. In another bowl, with a wire whisk, beat the eggs, milk, oil, and vanilla until smooth. Let the mixture stand 5 minutes to thicken.

3. Heat a nonstick crêpe pan or a heavy 8-inch skillet over medium heat; lightly coat with vegetable-oil cooking spray. Ladle a scant 1/4-cup batter into the skillet; tilt the pan, covering the bottom with batter and creating a 6-inch circle. Cook the crêpe until the top has set and is lighter in color, about 2 minutes. Carefully turn and briefly cook the other side. Transfer the crêpe to a sheet of waxed paper. Repeat with the remaining batters, stacking crêpes between sheets of waxed paper. Set aside until ready to serve.

4. **prepare raspberry sauce** In the bowl of a food processor fitted with the chopping blade, purée the raspberries, granulated sugar, and brandy, if desired, until smooth. Transfer the mixture to a fine strainer set over the bowl of an airtight container. With the back of a spoon, press the purée through the strainer; discard the pulp and seeds. Cover and refrigerate the sauce until ready to use.

5. **prepare banana-cream filling** Place the heavy cream, cream cheese, and confectioners' sugar in a medium bowl. With an electric mixer on high speed, beat until stiff peaks form. In another medium bowl, mix together the bananas and cinnamon. Fold 1 cup whipped cream into the banana mixture, then fold the banana mixture into the remaining whipped cream until the ingredients are well combined.

6. Defrost the crêpes if they have been frozen. When ready to serve, warm the crêpes in the microwave and place 1/3 cup filling in the center of each one. Fold both sides of the crêpe toward the center, covering the filling. Arrange the crêpes on a plate and drizzle with Raspberry Sauce.

Christmas bread

Makes 12 servings

Here is the grand finale to breakfast—a sugary, warm-from-the-oven, cinnamon-scented, orange-glazed bread shaped into a Christmas tree.

bread

Two 1-pound packages frozen white bread dough

1 large egg, beaten

1/2 cup granulated sugar

1 teaspoon ground cinnamon

2 tablespoons butter, melted

orange glaze

1 1/4 cups confectioners' sugar

2 tablespoons grated orange rind

3 to 4 tablespoons orange juice

1. **prepare dough** Place the frozen dough in a large oiled bowl, cover, and refrigerate overnight. Remove from the refrigerator, and let the dough rest in a warm place until it is doubled in size. This will take several hours. Punch the dough down and turn it onto a lightly floured surface. Divide the dough into 23 walnut-size balls.

2. **make tree shape** Preheat oven to 350°F. Grease a large nonstick baking sheet. Arrange balls of dough on the baking sheet in the shape of a Christmas tree: 2 balls for the trunk, 6 across for the bottom row of branches, then 5, 4, 3, 2, and 1 at the top, allowing the balls to touch one another. Brush the dough with egg and allow to rise until doubled in size, 20 to 25 minutes.

3. In a small bowl, combine the granulated sugar and cinnamon. Generously brush the dough tree with melted butter. Sprinkle cinnamon sugar evenly over the top. Bake until golden brown, 15 to 20 minutes. Transfer the baking sheet to a wire rack set over a piece of waxed paper; let the bread cool 10 minutes. Transfer the bread to the rack.

4. **prepare orange glaze** In a medium bowl, combine the confectioners' sugar, orange rind, and enough orange juice to attain a fairly runny consistency. Drizzle orange glaze over the bread. Serve the Christmas bread warm.

warm spiced cider

Makes 8 servings

Spicy cider is a good counterpoint to the rich dishes of this meal, a tasty beverage the family will appreciate.

8 cups apple cider

1/4 cup sugar

1 orange, thinly sliced

1 lemon, thinly sliced

1 lime, thinly sliced

Two 3-inch cinnamon sticks

12 whole allspice berries

8 whole cloves

Orange slices, for garnish

Cinnamon sticks, for garnish

1. **make cider** In a 3-quart saucepan, combine all the ingredients. Simmer over low heat, stirring occasionally, for 25 minutes; do not boil. Strain the mixture and discard the solids. Garnish with orange slices and cinnamon sticks. Serve hot.

intimate
GATHERING

A simple yet **sumptuous sit-down dinner** lets family and friends enjoy **an evening of festive** food and drink, holiday cheer, and good chat.

Hosting an intimate holiday dinner at home is a gesture that guests will remember fondly. The season is packed with parties and community celebrations, yet too rarely do we get a chance to enjoy a full evening with family and friends. Dinner doesn't have to be an elaborate affair. Try to limit the number of guests to eight; vary the personalities to ensure lively conversation. Treat your visitors to a beautiful table, but put them at ease by serving a simple buffet. Line the walkway and driveway with candelarias. As people arrive, play holiday music, open a bottle of wine, and let the festive spirit of the season take care of the rest of the evening.

A sit-down dinner is especially elegant when the table is set with your most cherished objects and bowls of freshly cut flowers. Creating an ambitious centerpiece absorbs vast amount of time and patience. Instead, parade smaller, intimate bouquets in your collectible pottery along the table.

elegant
casual...

Christmas is the perfect time to revisit collections. A holiday party seems the most celebratory when we bring out all those heirloom linens and showcase Grandmother's silver. After all, what are you saving it for, if not Christmas? Still, when you plan your gathering, toss casual elements in the mix. Flea-market vases, candleholders, and serving pieces contribute a stylish yet easygoing mood.

Greenery collected from your own backyard can decorate serving tables and form natural bobeches for candles (above). Ironstone bowls and tureens (opposite) transform an old white-painted sideboard into a composed buffet. Orchids in winter-white pots reinforce the color scheme, while pears and juniper branches offer fresh touches of green.

Spreading out dinner on a sideboard will encourage guests to relax. At a buffet, folks mingle as they fill their plates. You too get to visit more with friends. When selecting the menu, consider the colors of the foods. Our festive buffet features a green bean salad with golden pears and roasted vegetables with red, orange, and yellow bell peppers. Showcased in creamy ironstone bowls, the dishes are dramatic.

Any room can have

an inviting atmosphere.

The tools: soft colors, favorite pieces, fresh greens.

A palette of white and pale green is a breath of fresh air in dreary winter. We've enlisted pieces from collections of creamware, milk glass, McCoy pottery, and jadeite to serve as vases. The tulips, roses, narcissus, and ranunculus that fill them are all beautiful winter-white bouquets.

Bring in outdoor beauty with ivy, boxwood, and juniper topiaries. Tuck greenery behind picture frames, around mirrors, and on the table. Give the dining room its very own Christmas tree, with demure glass balls and sparkling white lights.

Drape your table in white linen, the finest you can find. For this meal only, iron out every wrinkle and center the cloth exactly. The unifying white motif will allow for a rustic mix of chairs.

Even an intimate holiday dinner should

have pretty place cards to welcome guests at the table.

The best place cards are treats to take home.

A candle at each place setting (above) bathes the table with light. We've tied a simple red tag to a Victorian Christmas light, but a contemporary votive would work just as well. Prior to the advent of electric Christmas bulbs, these colorful glass containers were fitted with candles and hung from evergreens or the eaves of a house.

A lady apple is a naturally elegant place marker. Stencil or stamp a name tag in pale red and green (opposite top) and tie it to the stem of the fruit with cord or narrow ribbon. You can also make a small slit in the top of a perfect apple or pear to hold the place card.

Vintage holiday cards with their wintry scenes (opposite below) will encourage everyone to reminisce about a white Christmas. Be on the lookout for good cards at summer flea markets. Photocopy a favorite image, mount it on card stock, and adapt a pinecone as a card holder.

A potted holiday flower at each seat is a perfect example of place holder and party favor in one. Label plant markers with guests' names and poke them into the soil.

warm pear &
green bean salad

cannellini-bean soup
with sage pesto

PERFECT PAIR Sweet pears and garden-fresh green beans may seem like an unlikely match, but they blend beautifully in a holiday salad. The pears and beans are simply roasted in the oven, tossed with a light dressing, and topped with toasted hazelnuts. The salad can be served warm or at room temperature, for a buffet-style meal as well as a sit-down dinner.

WARM AND CREAMY Chase away all the chill of winter with a single bowl of creamy, hearty cannellini-bean soup. Swirl sage pesto on each serving to bring out color and flavor. The soup is convenient because it can be made up to three days in advance, stored in the refrigerator, and warmed on the evening of the party. Sage pesto takes only minutes to prepare.

roasted vegetables

WINTER COLOR Just because the weather's dreary, food doesn't have to be. Roasted vegetables are a lively dish on any holiday menu. The vegetables include vibrant strips of red, orange, and yellow bell peppers as well as brussels sprouts, red potatoes, fennel, and cipollini onions. Of course, you can adapt the ingredients to suit your family's favorites.

CROWD PLEASER An herb-crusted pork roast is sure to be a popular treat, and the leftovers—if there are any—make terrific sandwiches. A boneless pork loin will handily serve a party of eight. To intensify the flavor, the pork is coated with Dijon mustard, orange juice, and grated orange zest before it's roasted. Garnish the platter with kumquats for a burst of color.

herb-crusted
boneless pork roast

warm pear & green bean salad

Makes 8 servings

We all save a spot for something healthful, and this salad provides vegetable and fruit in one dish.

Vegetable-oil cooking spray
1/4 cup extra virgin olive oil
1 teaspoon salt
1/2 teaspoon ground black pepper
2 pounds green beans, trimmed
4 pears, cored and cut into eighths
1 teaspoon sugar
1/2 cup chopped toasted hazelnuts

dressing

2 tablespoons sherry wine vinegar
1 teaspoon Dijon-style mustard
1/2 teaspoon minced garlic
1/4 cup extra virgin olive oil
1/4 teaspoon salt
1/4 teaspoon ground black pepper

1. **roast vegetables** Preheat the oven to 400°F. Lightly coat two roasting pans with cooking spray and set aside. In a large bowl, whisk 2 table-spoons oil, 1/2 teaspoon salt, and 1/4 teaspoon pepper. Toss the beans well with this mixture and place them in a roasting pan. In the same large bowl, whisk the remaining oil, salt, and pepper and toss with the pears. Sprinkle the pears with sugar and place them in the second roasting pan. Place both pans in the oven. After 30 minutes remove the green beans. Roast the pears 15 more minutes and remove from the oven.

2. **prepare dressing** In a small bowl, whisk together the vinegar, mustard, and garlic. Add the olive oil in a thin stream, whisking constantly until the mixture is emulsified. Whisk in the salt and pepper. In a salad bowl, toss together the beans, pears, and dressing. Serve immediately.

cannellini-bean soup with sage pesto

Makes 8 servings

The ingredients may be humble indeed but cannellini soup with sage pesto is a treat any gourmet will praise. With garlic bread, it's a marvelous supper.

6 cloves garlic
1 tablespoon extra virgin olive oil
1 cup chopped onion
2 shallots, peeled and chopped
Two 14 1/2-ounce cans reduced-sodium chicken broth
Four 19-ounce cans cannellini beans with liquid
1 teaspoon salt
1/2 teaspoon ground black pepper
2 tablespoons half-and-half
Sage Pesto (recipe follows)

1. Heat the oven to 400°F. Wrap the garlic cloves in aluminum foil and roast for 30 minutes. Remove from the oven and set aside.

2. **prepare soup** In a 6-quart saucepan, heat the oil and sauté the onion and shallots until softened, about 10 minutes. Stir in the broth, beans, salt, and pepper. Simmer 20 minutes. Squeeze the roasted garlic from its papery skin into the soup. Puree the mixture in batches in a blender or food processor until it is smooth. Return the soup to the saucepan and stir in the half-and-half. Serve the soup with 2 teaspoons Sage Pesto swirled into each serving.

sage pesto

3 tablespoons chopped fresh sage
2 cloves garlic
1/4 cup grated Parmesan cheese
1/2 teaspoon salt
1/4 teaspoon ground black pepper
2 tablespoons chopped fresh parsley
1/4 cup chopped walnuts
1/2 cup extra virgin olive oil

1. Place all the ingredients except the oil in a blender or food processor fitted with a metal blade; process until the ingredients are well-combined. Slowly add the olive oil and process until the pesto is smooth.

herb-crusted boneless pork roast

Makes 8 servings

Place this crowning achievement on the table and you may well receive a round of applause. You deserve it; this is one delicious pork roast.

Vegetable-oil cooking spray

1/4 cup Dijon-style mustard

1 tablespoon orange juice

1 teaspoon grated orange zest

One 3- to 3 1/2-pound boneless pork loin

1 1/2 teaspoons chopped fresh rosemary

1 teaspoon chopped fresh sage

1 clove garlic, minced

1 teaspoon salt

1/2 teaspoon ground black pepper

1. **roast pork** Preheat the oven to 425°F. Lightly coat a rack placed in a roasting pan with cooking spray. In a small bowl, whisk the mustard, orange juice, and zest. Spread the mixture over the surface of the pork loin and place it on the wire rack. Roast the pork on the middle rack of the oven for 30 minutes.

2. **make crust** In a small bowl, toss the rosemary, sage, garlic, salt, and pepper. Remove the pork from the oven and pat the herb mixture onto the top and sides. Reduce the oven temperature to 350°F and continue to roast the pork until a meat thermometer inserted into the center of the roast registers 160°F, about 45 minutes longer.

3. Remove the pork roast from the oven and allow it to rest 15 minutes before serving. Carve the roast and serve warm.

roasted garden vegetables

Makes 8 servings

Vegetables in season always taste best, and winter vegetables have a richness that summer's lighter, juicier fare can't match. Oven roasting brings out all the deep flavors. If you can't find cipollini onions, substitute white pearl ones.

3 tablespoons extra virgin olive oil

1 pound cipollini onions, peeled

1 1/2 pounds small red potatoes, quartered

1 large fennel bulb, trimmed and cut lengthwise into 1/2-inch chunks

1 pint brussels sprouts

2 large red bell peppers, cut into thick strips

1 large yellow bell pepper, cut into thick strips

1 large orange bell pepper, cut into thick strips

dressing

3/4 cup balsamic vinegar

2 teaspoons sugar

3 cloves garlic, minced

1 1/2 teaspoons salt

1/2 teaspoon black pepper

1. **roast vegetables** Preheat the oven to 425°F. Combine the olive oil, onions, and potatoes in a large bowl and toss to coat on all sides. Put the vegetables in a roasting pan and roast 10 minutes. Add the fennel and brussels sprouts to the cipollini and potatoes and roast 10 more minutes. Add the red, yellow, and orange peppers and continue to roast, stirring occasionally, until all the vegetables are tender, about 20 minutes.

2. **make dressing** In a small saucepan, combine the vinegar and sugar and bring to a boil. Continue to cook until the mixture is reduced to 3 tablespoons. Add the garlic, salt, and pepper to the balsamic mixture and drizzle it over the vegetables. Toss to coat. Serve the vegetables warm or at room temperature.

gingerbread cake
with white-chocolate buttercream

pumpkin-nutmeg flan

DELICIOUS GIFT Present your guests with a gift that becomes even sweeter when it's shared among friends—a four-layer gingerbread cake wrapped in fluffy white-chocolate buttercream and topped with lengths of chocolate ribbon. If you make the layers ahead of time, all you'll have to do on the day of the party is whip up the buttercream and frost the cake.

SPICE IT UP An interesting dessert buffet includes a variety of shapes, colors, and textures. A pumpkin-nutmeg flan is drizzled with caramel and topped with ruby-red pomegranate seeds for a touch of color. For a full buffet, we've also created recipes for Almond Sugar Cookies, Chunky Chocolate-Chip Cookies, Ginger Cider, and Candy-Bar Hot Chocolate.

gingerbread cake

Makes 24 servings

Everyone craves gingerbread at Christmas, but we've dolled it up. This reliable standby is transformed into what may be the holiday's most glamorous dessert.

Vegetable-oil cooking spray
1 cup (2 sticks) unsalted butter, softened
1 cup light brown sugar
4 large eggs
2 teaspoons grated orange zest
5 cups all-purpose flour
4 teaspoons baking soda
5 teaspoons ground ginger
2 teaspoons cinnamon
1 teaspoon ground allspice
1 teaspoon ground nutmeg
1 teaspoon salt
1/2 teaspoon ground cloves
2 cups boiling water
1 1/2 cups molasses
1/2 cup orange juice
White-Chocolate Buttercream (recipe follows)
Chocolate Ribbon (recipe follows)

1. **prepare cake** Preheat the oven to 350°F. Lightly coat four 9-inch square cake pans with cooking spray and set aside. In the large bowl of an electric mixer, beat the butter on medium-high speed for 3 minutes. Add the sugar and continue to beat until the mixture is light and fluffy, about 3 minutes. Reduce the speed to low and add the eggs, one at a time, scraping down the side of the bowl after each addition. Mix in the grated orange zest and set aside.

2. In a large mixing bowl, combine the flour, baking soda, ginger, cinnamon, allspice, nutmeg, salt, and cloves. Set aside.

3. Pour the boiling water, molasses, and orange juice into a 4-cup glass measure or medium bowl. Set aside.

4. **make batter** With the mixer on low speed, add one third of the flour mixture to the butter mixture. Add one third of the molasses mixture. Continue alternating until all the ingredients are combined, scraping down the side of the bowl occasionally. Divide the batter evenly among the cake pans. Bake the cakes until a toothpick inserted in the center of each comes out clean, 20 to 25 minutes. Cool the cakes in the pans on wire racks 5 minutes, then remove the pans. Let the layers rest on racks until completely cooled.

5. **frost cake** Place a cooled cake layer on a serving plate and spread two-thirds cup White-Chocolate Buttercream over the layer. Top with the next layer and more buttercream, repeating for the remaining layers. Spread a thin layer of buttercream over the assembled layers. Chill for 20 minutes. Frost the top and sides of the cake with the remaining buttercream.

6. Crisscross the ribbons over the cake. Refrigerate until 30 minutes before serving.

white-chocolate buttercream

Makes 8 cups

12 egg whites
1/2 cup granulated sugar
2 1/4 cups unsalted butter, softened
18 ounces white chocolate, melted and cooled to room temperature

1. **make buttercream** In a 3-quart saucepan, boil 3 cups water and reduce to a slow simmer. Place the egg whites and sugar in a large heat-proof bowl over simmering water, making sure the bottom of the bowl does not touch the water. Whisk the mixture by hand or on low speed until the sugar dissolves and mixture is very hot to the touch, 7 to 10 minutes.

2. Remove the bowl from heat and beat at high speed with an electric mixer until the whites are glossy and thoroughly cooked, 7 to 10 minutes.

3. Add the butter to the egg white meringue, 2 tablespoons at a time, until it is incorporated. As butter is added, the frosting may appear

curdled. This is normal; the frosting will become smooth and glossy again just by continuing to beat it. Add the white chocolate and beat until the frosting is fluffy, about 5 minutes.

chocolate ribbon

Makes 5 ounces

4 ounces semisweet chocolate, chopped
3 tablespoons light corn syrup
1 tablespoon cocoa powder, for work surface

1. **prepare chocolate** In a 3-quart saucepan, bring 3 cups water to a boil and reduce to a slow simmer. Place the chocolate in a medium mixing bowl and set the bowl over simmering water, making sure the bottom of the bowl does not touch the water. Stir the chocolate until it is melted. Remove the bowl from the heat.

2. Stir the corn syrup into the melted chocolate until thoroughly blended and the mixture forms a soft ball. Wrap the chocolate in plastic and allow to stand at room temperature until the mixture reaches the consistency of modeling clay, about 30 minutes. (If you are preparing the chocolate a day ahead, wrap it tightly in plastic and store it at room temperature. To use, knead the wrapped chocolate until it is pliable.)

3. **form ribbon** Remove plastic wrap and sprinkle the work surface with cocoa powder. Roll out the chocolate into a narrow rectangle 1/4- to 1/8-inch thick. With a pastry wheel or the tip of a sharp knife, cut 2 strips of ribbon, each about 13 inches long and 1 inch wide. Cut a V-shape from each end of the ribbons.

pumpkin-nutmeg flan

Makes 8 servings

Call it what you will—flan, custard, creme brulée, panna cotta, pudding…the whole family of creamy baked desserts is beloved around the world. Cooks rely on them to bring a sweet ending to any meal; diners always find room for some, regardless of how much they've eaten. Try this special Christmas version.

Vegetable-oil cooking spray
1/2 cup sugar
1/4 cup water
1/8 teaspoon grated nutmeg
One 15-ounce can pumpkin puree
1/2 cup packed light brown sugar
1 tablespoon cornstarch
1/4 teaspoon salt
1/2 teaspoon pumpkin-pie spice
3 large eggs
1 cup milk
1 teaspoon vanilla extract
1/2 cup pomegranate seeds

1. **make caramel** Preheat the oven to 350°F. Spray a 6-cup metal ring mold with cooking spray and set aside. In a small saucepan over medium heat, combine the sugar and water and cook until the mixture is golden brown, 6 to 8 minutes. Do not stir. Immediately pour the caramel into the prepared ring mold and tip the mold to allow the syrup to coat the bottom. Sprinkle nutmeg over the syrup and set the ring mold aside.

2. **make flan** In a food processor fitted with a metal blade, combine the pumpkin, sugar, cornstarch, salt, pumpkin-pie spice, eggs, milk, and vanilla. Pour the mixture into the ring mold, cover with aluminum foil, and place in a roasting pan. Pour hot tap water around the mold to a depth of 1 inch. Bake until the flan is set, about one hour. Remove the mold from the roasting pan, uncover, and cool on a wire rack. Cover the flan and refrigerate several hours or overnight.

3. **to serve** Uncover the flan and loosen the edges with a table knife. Dip the mold in a bowl of hot water for 1 minute to loosen. Invert the flan onto cake plate, allowing carmel syrup to drizzle onto the flan. Garnish with pomegranate seeds.

almond sugar cookies

Makes 2 dozen

Versatile barely begins to describe these terrific cookies. They can be served as-is, of course, but try them sandwiched with warm jam, dipped in chocolate, or dusted with confectioners' sugar or cocoa.

Vegetable-oil cooking spray

3 cups flour

3 teaspoons baking powder

1/2 teaspoon salt

1 cup sugar

6 tablespoons butter, softened

6 tablespoons vegetable shortening

3 eggs, separated

1 1/2 teaspoons almond extract

1/4 cup orange juice

1 cup sliced almonds

1. **prepare dough** Preheat the oven to 350°F. Lightly coat 2 large baking sheets with cooking spray. Set aside. Sift the flour, baking powder, salt, and sugar into a large mixing bowl. Cut in the butter and vegetable shortening with a pastry blender or two knives until it resembles coarse meal. Mix in the egg yolks.

2. In a medium bowl, beat the egg whites and the almond extract with an electric mixer on medium-high speed until soft peaks form, about 3 minutes. Gently fold the whites into the dough. Mix in the orange juice.

3. **cut dough** Turn the dough out onto a lightly floured surface and knead briefly until it comes together and is smooth, about 2 minutes. Roll out the dough into a 9- by 12-inch rectangle about 1/2 inch thick. With a fluted pastry cutter or a sharp knife, cut the 12-inch length of the rectangle to divide it into four 3-inch-wide strips. Cut each strip into four 3-inch squares. Cut along the diagonal of each square to form 24 triangles.

4. **bake cookies** Place the dough triangles on a baking sheet and sprinkle almonds over each one. Press the almonds lightly into the dough. Bake the cookies until the edges are lightly browned, 7 to 10 minutes. Remove the cookies from the baking sheet and cool on a wire rack.

chunky chocolate-chip cookies

Makes 2 dozen

So what if we can have chocolate chip cookies all year round? That doesn't mean we should forget them at Christmas.

Vegetable-oil cooking spray

4 1/2 cups all-purpose flour

1 teaspoon salt

1 teaspoon baking soda

1 1/2 cups (3 sticks) unsalted butter, melted and cooled

2 cups firmly packed dark brown sugar

1 cup granulated sugar

2 large eggs

1 egg yolk

1 1/2 tablespoons vanilla extract

2 cups semisweet chocolate chips

1 cup bittersweet chocolate, coarsely chopped

1 cup chopped walnuts

1. **make dough** Preheat the oven to 350°F. Lightly coat two large baking sheets with cooking spray. Set aside. In a large mixing bowl, whisk together the flour, salt, and baking soda. In a medium bowl, combine the cooled butter, brown sugar, and granulated sugar. Whisk in the eggs, egg yolk, and vanilla. Stir the butter mixture into the flour mixture. Fold in the chocolate chips, chopped chocolate, and walnuts.

2. **bake cookies** With a dry measuring cup, scoop one-third cup dough for each cookie and shape into a ball. Place the balls on prepared baking sheets, leaving 2 inches of space between each. Bake until the edges are lightly browned and the centers are set, 20 to 25 minutes. Cool the cookies on wire racks.

ginger cider

Makes 8 servings

Vary the flavor of this comforting cider by pouring in some cranberry juice cocktail, Concord grape juice, or a bit of prune juice.

1/2 gallon apple cider

1/3 cup dark brown sugar

2 sticks cinnamon

5 whole allspice berries

1 chunk fresh ginger, 1/2 inch by 1/2 inch, peeled

3 whole cloves

8 orange slices

1. In a 3-quart saucepan, combine the cider, sugar, cinnamon sticks, allspice berries, ginger, and cloves. Heat to a simmer and allow to cook 20 minutes. Strain the cider into a punch bowl and garnish with orange slices. Serve warm.

candy-bar hot chocolate

Makes 8 servings

In Europe, hot chocolate is made from chocolate, not cocoa. The extra-intense flavor makes this a treat to be sipped and savored from demitasse cups.

One 8-ounce dark bittersweet or semisweet chocolate bar

1/2 cup heavy cream

2 quarts milk

Whipped cream

1. In a 3-quart saucepan, combine the chocolate and heavy cream. Stir over medium heat until the chocolate melts. Whisk in the milk and heat until the mixture is hot but not boiling, about 7 minutes. Pour the chocolate into cups and garnish with whipped cream.

a sweet sugarplum
FINALE

Nothing says Christmas more than a tantalizing array of cookies and cakes, tortes and tarts, and pastries. Guests will stand in line for dessert.

Everyone's favorite part of a holiday gathering is the sweet finale. No matter how delicious the meal, we all save room for dessert. This holiday season, consider hosting a dessert party instead of a conventional dinner. It can be the perfect way to entertain neighbors, coworkers, or a group of parents after a school play. Here is a rule of thumb for planning the menu: Each guest will probably eat four cookies and one small piece of each cake and tart. If you want to host a kids-only afternoon, invite a crew over to make a gingerbread house, or an entire village. Children of all ages can join in on the fun, and the season will be off to a very sweet start.

To enliven the spread at a dessert party, display the sweets—such as Christmas cake and ricotta cheesecake—at different levels with a variety of cake stands and platters. Mercury-glass candleholders, glass balls, and ruby-color goblets bring more sparkle and shine to the scene.

season of sweets...

We all remember the heavenly aroma of sugar cookies baking in the oven every Christmas season. While this favorite remains unbeatable, it's still fun to try new recipes. Our dessert buffet offers sweets that would be perfect for an informal gathering as well as an elegant soirée—tiny pecan tarts filled with nutty caramel, raspberry-walnut rugelach in a flaky cream-cheese pastry, and buttery poppyseed crescents dusted with confectioners' sugar.

No dessert buffet would be complete without a selection of beautifully dressed cakes. Golden Ricotta Cheesecake is topped with tangy orange slices, while the Chocolate Espresso Torte wears a bouquet of sugared cranberries and chocolate leaves. All you need is Champagne or a dessert wine to top off the evening, and plenty of mineral water for cleansing palates.

Arranging desserts on several tables will allow guests to meander about, sampling your buffet fare throughout the evening. Devote one station (opposite) to coffee, tea, and a selection of delectable cookies. If your family is among the millions that consider a gingerbread house essential, present them with this one (above).

chocolate espresso torte

DRESSED TO THRILL A chocolate torte serves as the belle of the table, thanks to its elegant corsage. Within its ganache glaze is a dense chocolate cake flavored with espresso. Small portions, please; this is one of the richest desserts we've ever created. Decorations may be gilding the lily, but the torte can be trimmed with fresh berries and chocolate leaves or curls.

YOUNG AT HEART If you're planning to have children at your dessert party, give them their very own table with kid-friendly sweets and glasses of cold milk. Colorful sugar cookies are always a hit, and Mint Sandwich Cookies just might become a new family favorite. Chocolate coins wrapped in silver and gold are a traditional Hanukkah treat.

Christmas cake

Makes 12 servings

This fruity cake, inspired by English plum puddings, may be garnished with whipped cream.

> 1 cup all-purpose flour
>
> 1 teaspoon ground cinnamon
>
> 3/4 teaspoon baking powder
>
> 1/2 teaspoon salt
>
> 1/2 teaspoon freshly ground nutmeg
>
> 4 cups fresh white bread crumbs
>
> 1/2 cup dried plums, chopped
>
> 1/2 cup golden raisins
>
> 1 cup dried figs, coarsely chopped
>
> 1/2 cup dried cranberries
>
> 1 cup firmly packed light brown sugar
>
> 3 large eggs, lightly beaten
>
> 1/2 cup (1 stick) unsalted butter, melted
>
> 1/3 cup honey
>
> 1/2 cup Grand Marnier or dark rum
>
> 1 tablespoon grated orange zest
>
> 1 1/2 teaspoons vanilla extract

1. Generously butter a 2-quart steamed pudding mold. Fit a large covered pot deep enough to hold the pudding mold with a wire rack.

2. **make batter** In a large bowl, sift the flour, cinnamon, baking powder, salt, and nutmeg. Toss together the bread crumbs, dried plums, raisins, figs, and cranberries. Whisk together the remaining ingredients and stir into the dry ingredients.

3. Pour the batter into the mold, snap on the lid, and cover the top with foil. Place the mold on the rack in the pot and fill the pot halfway up the side of the mold with very hot water. Cover the pot and bring the water to a simmer.

4. **steam pudding** Steam the pudding until a tester inserted into the center comes out clean, about 5 hours. Add boiling water to maintain water level during the steaming process.

5. Transfer the mold to a rack and cool for 30 minutes. Unmold pudding and cool on the rack. Serve warm, cut in slender slices.

ricotta cheesecake

Makes 12 servings

So many densely heavy desserts turn up during the holidays; as a break, try this light cheesecake.

> 1 1/4 cups shortbread cookie crumbs
>
> 4 tablespoons butter, melted
>
> 1/4 cup sugar
>
> 1 cup golden raisins
>
> 24 ounces ricotta cheese
>
> 1/4 cup pine nuts, toasted
>
> 1 tablespoon grated orange zest
>
> 3 large eggs
>
> 3/4 cup sugar
>
> 1 teaspoon vanilla extract

1. **make crust** Preheat the oven to 350°F. In a medium bowl, combine the cookie crumbs, butter, and sugar. Press the mixture into a 9- or 10-inch springform pan and bake for 10 minutes, until the crust is set. Set aside.

2. **make filling** In a medium bowl, pour boiling water over the raisins to cover and let stand for 5 minutes; drain. In a large bowl, combine the raisins, ricotta cheese, toasted pine nuts, and zest. In another large bowl, using a mixer set on medium speed, beat the eggs, about 2 minutes. Add sugar and vanilla and beat until thick, about 2 minutes. Reduce the speed to low, add the ricotta mixture, and mix until combined. Pour the filling into the prepared crust.

3. **bake cheesecake** Place the cheesecake on the center rack of the oven and bake until the top is golden brown and the center of the cake jiggles slightly, 50 to 60 minutes. Cool the cake on the rack for 2 hours. Cover with plastic wrap and chill for several hours. Unmold to serve.

chocolate espresso torte

Tempted by desserts called "Death by Chocolate" or "Chocolate Sin"? This is the torte for you.

21 ounces semisweet chocolate, chopped

1 1/2 cups (3 sticks) unsalted butter

2 tablespoons powdered espresso or coffee crystals

5 large eggs, separated

3/4 cup sugar

1 tablespoon vanilla extract

1/2 cup all-purpose flour

1/4 teaspoon salt

1/2 teaspoon cream of tartar

1 tablespoon light corn syrup

2 tablespoons heavy cream

1. **make batter** Preheat oven to 350°F. Butter a 9-inch square cake pan and line the bottom with parchment paper. Butter the paper.

2. In the top of a double boiler, over low heat, melt together 9 ounces chocolate and 3/4 cup butter. Remove the mixture from the heat and set aside.

3. In a large bowl, using a mixer set on medium speed, beat the egg yolks until foamy, 15 to 30 seconds. Add 1/2 cup of the sugar and continue to beat until the mixture is thick and pale, 3 to 5 minutes. Reduce the mixer speed to low and add the chocolate mixture, vanilla, flour, and salt.

4. In a medium bowl, using a mixer set on medium speed, beat the egg whites and cream of tartar to soft peaks. Add the remaining sugar in a thin stream and beat until stiff peaks form. Fold the whites into the chocolate mixture by thirds.

5. **bake cake** Pour the batter into the prepared pan and bake until a toothpick inserted in the center of cake comes out clean, about 35 minutes. Cool the cake for 30 minutes. Invert the cake onto a wire rack set over a baking sheet.

6. **make glaze** In a double boiler over low heat, melt the remaining 12 ounces of chocolate. Remove the melted chocolate from the heat and stir in the softened butter until combined. Stir in the corn syrup and heavy cream. Allow the mixture to cool until the glaze is thick enough to coat yet still pours easily, 2 to 3 minutes.

7. Pour the glaze onto the center of the cake and use a metal spatula to smooth it evenly over the top and sides. Allow the glaze to set for 10 minutes. Carefully transfer the torte to a serving platter.

mint sandwich cookies

The only problem kids will have with these cookies is whether to eat the cookie or the filling first.

1 cup all-purpose flour

1 tablespoon unsweetened cocoa powder

1/2 cup (1 stick) cold butter, cut into 8 pieces

1/2 cup heavy cream

1 1/2 cups plus 2 tablespoons confectioners' sugar

6 tablespoons unsalted butter, softened

1 teaspoon vanilla extract

16 thin chocolate mints, finely chopped

1. **make cookie dough** In the bowl of a food processor fitted with a metal blade, pulse to combine the flour, cocoa powder, and the cold butter until it resembles a coarse meal. With the processor running, add 1/4 cup of the heavy cream in a steady stream and process until a dough forms. Remove the dough and shape it into a disk; wrap in plastic wrap and chill 1 hour.

2. Preheat oven to 375°F. Line a baking sheet with parchment paper and set aside. Lightly dust work surface with 2 tablespoons confectioners' sugar and roll the dough out to 1/8-inch thickness. With a 1 1/4-inch round cutter, cut out the cookies and place them on a baking sheet. Use a fork to prick 3 rows of holes into each cookie.

3. **bake cookies** Bake the cookies until firm to the touch, 8 to 10 minutes. Remove and transfer the cookies to a wire rack to cool completely.

4. **make filling** In a small bowl, with a mixer on medium speed, cream the butter and the remaining sugar. Add the remaining cream and the vanilla and beat until smooth. Stir in the mints.

5. **assemble cookies** Place 2 teaspoons filling between 2 cookies to make a sandwich. Repeat with the remaining cookies.

simple sugar cookies

Makes 4 dozen

Call the kids into the kitchen to bake and decorate these; pull out all your Christmas cookie cutters.

2 cups (4 sticks) unsalted butter, at room temperature

1 1/4 cups granulated sugar

2 large eggs

2 large egg yolks

2 teaspoons vanilla extract

5 cups all-purpose flour

1/2 teaspoon salt

3/4 teaspoon nutmeg

1 large egg white

Colored sugars for sprinkling

1. **make dough** In a large bowl using a mixer set on medium speed, cream the butter until light and fluffy. Slowly add the granulated sugar and beat until combined. Add the eggs, the yolks, and the vanilla and mix thoroughly. Reduce the speed to medium low. Add the flour, salt, and nutmeg, and mix until combined. Divide the dough in half, shape each piece in a 6- by 4-inch rectangle, and wrap in plastic. Chill for 4 to 24 hours.

2. Preheat oven to 350°F. Line two baking sheets with parchment paper and set aside. On a lightly floured surface, roll out the dough to 1/8-inch thickness. Cut out shapes and, using a spatula to

transfer them, place the cutouts 2 inches apart on the prepared baking sheets.

3. **bake cookies** Lightly brush the cookies with egg white. Sprinkle them with colored sugar, and shake off any excess sugar. Bake until the cookies are golden brown, about 15 minutes, rotating pans halfway through. Gather up the dough scraps, shape them into a disk, and chill again. Repeat shaping cookies.

tiny pecan tarts

Makes 24

We adapted Southern pecan pie into tarts made with a cream-cheese pastry, for a perfect Christmas dessert.

1/2 cup plus 1 1/2 tablespoons unsalted butter, softened

One 3-ounce package cream cheese, softened

1 cup all-purpose flour

1 1/2 tablespoons honey

1/4 cup light brown sugar

2 1/2 tablespoons granulated sugar

1/8 teaspoon salt

1 cup coarsely chopped pecans

2 1/2 tablespoons heavy cream

1. **make tart dough** Preheat the oven to 350°F. In a medium bowl using a mixer set on medium speed, beat 1/2 cup butter and the cream cheese together until smooth. Add the flour and blend until a soft dough forms. Shape the dough into a disk, wrap in plastic, and chill for 30 minutes.

2. Divide the dough into 24 equal-size balls and press each into the cup of a mini-muffin pan to form a shell. Bake until the pastry is golden brown, 20 to 25 minutes. Cool the tarts in the pan for 10 minutes, then transfer to a wire rack.

3. **fill shells** In a saucepan over medium heat, combine the honey, sugars, remaining butter, and salt. Bring to a boil and cook 3 minutes. Stir in the pecans and cream. Remove the mixture from the heat and let cool for 10 minutes. Spoon the filling into the prepared shells.

raspberry-walnut rugelach

Makes 24 cookies

Raspberry, walnuts, and cream cheese: They feature prominently in this heavenly rugelach.

- 1 pound cream cheese, softened
- 1 cup (2 sticks) unsalted butter, softened
- 1/2 teaspoon salt
- 2 teaspoons vanilla extract
- 2 cups all-purpose flour
- 1/2 cup raisins, coarsely chopped
- 1 cup finely chopped walnuts
- 1/2 cup light brown sugar
- 1 teaspoon ground cinnamon
- 3/4 cup seedless raspberry jam
- 1 large egg, beaten
- 2 tablespoons granulated sugar

1. **make dough** In a large bowl, beat the cream cheese, butter, salt, and vanilla until smooth. Add the flour and mix until just blended. Divide the dough in half; wrap in plastic. Chill 3 hours.

2. Preheat the oven to 350°F. Line a baking sheet with parchment paper and set aside. In a medium bowl, combine the raisins, walnuts, brown sugar, and cinnamon and set aside.

3. On a lightly floured surface, roll out half the dough into a 9-inch circle. Spread half of the jam on the circle, leaving a 1/2-inch clean border. Sprinkle with 1/2 of the raisin mixture. Cut the circle into 12 equal-sized wedges. Beginning with the wide edge, roll wedges up to form cookies and place them 3 inches apart on the prepared baking sheet. Brush lightly with the beaten egg and sprinkle with sugar.

4. **bake rugelach** Bake the rugelach until it is golden brown and firm to the touch, 20 to 25 minutes. Remove the rugelach from the baking pan and transfer to a wire rack to cool. Repeat with the remaining dough.

lemon poppyseed crescents

Makes 30 cookies

Lemon crescents are popular in so many cultures and for good reason. The cookie dough is fun for little fingers to shape into crescents.

- 1 1/2 cups all-purpose flour
- 1/2 teaspoon salt
- 1/2 cup (1 stick) unsalted butter, softened
- One 3-ounce package cream cheese, softened
- 1/4 cup granulated sugar
- 1/2 teaspoon vanilla extract
- 1 tablespoon lemon zest
- 1/4 cup poppyseeds
- 3 tablespoons confectioners' sugar

1. **make dough** In a medium bowl, combine the flour and salt and set aside. In a large bowl with a mixer set on medium speed, beat the butter and cream cheese until well blended. Add the sugar and beat until light and fluffy, 1 minute. Stir in the vanilla and lemon zest until just blended.

2. Reduce the speed to low, add the flour and poppyseeds, and mix until a firm dough forms. Shape the dough into a disk, cover tightly with plastic wrap, and chill for 1 hour.

3. **shape crescents** Preheat the oven to 350°F. Line two baking sheets with parchment paper and set aside. Divide the dough into 30 equal-size pieces and form each piece into a crescent. Flatten each crescent slightly and place on a prepared baking sheet.

4. Bake the cookies until the edges are browned, about 25 minutes. Remove the cookies from the oven, immediately dust with confectioners' sugar, and transfer to a wire rack to cool completely.

gingerbread cottage

A Christmas gingerbread cottage will charm all your holiday visitors. Though it's made with "real" ingredients, the cottage is more for display than for eating (but it does have a rich fragrance). To begin, enlarge the templates on page 137 and transfer them to medium-gauge cardboard or foam core.

1 1/2 cups vegetable shortening

1 1/2 cups sugar

1 teaspoon salt

1 tablespoon cinnamon

2 teaspoons ground ginger

1 teaspoon ground cloves

1 teaspoon nutmeg

12 ounces unsulfured molasses

1 teaspoon vanilla extract

6 1/2 cups all purpose flour

Vegetable-oil cooking spray

1 **make dough** In a heavy-duty mixer fitted with the paddle attachment or in a large bowl with a hand mixer on medium speed, blend the vegetable shortening and the sugar until they are well combined. Add the salt and spices and continue to mix until the ingredients are incorporated. Scrape the side of the bowl. Add the vanilla and mix for 30 seconds. If you are using a heavy-duty mixer, add the flour one cup at a time. If you are working manually, stir in the flour with a wooden spoon, kneading the final cups of flour in by hand. Divide the dough into two 1 1/2-inch-thick squares. Wrap in plastic wrap and set aside.

2 **cut out shapes** Preheat the oven to 350°F. Between sheets of waxed or parchment paper, roll each dough half into a 12- by 16-inch rectangle, about 1/4 inch thick. Lightly coat roof, side, and front templates with cooking spray and position them on the dough. Cut around the outlines and windows of the templates. Remove the excess dough and set aside. Repeat the process, replacing the front with the back template.

3 **bake gingerbread** Carefully slide a sideless baking sheet under the parchment of one set of cut-out dough pieces. Repeat for the second set. Make sure that the dough lies completely flat. Bake until the gingerbread is firm but not hard to the touch, 20 to 25 minutes. Cool the gingerbread for 10 minutes and transfer to a wire rack to cool completely.

(continued on page 136)

royal icing

2 pounds confectioners' sugar

4 large egg whites

Red and green professional-strength
liquid-paste food colors

1 In a large bowl, mix the sugar and egg whites at medium speed until the
icing is smooth, glossy, and able to hold a distinct shape.

2 Divide the icing among three bowls. Tint one bowl red and another green.
Cover all three bowls tightly and set aside.

construction

20 multi-colored hard candies

One 10-inch heavy-gauge cardboard circle

Coarse white sugar crystals

4 miniature candy canes

1 battery-operated light

make stained-glass windows and doors

1 Preheat oven to 350°F. Place the baked gingerbread house sides, front, and
back on a parchment- or foil-lined baking sheet. In a food processor, pulse
to grind hard candy to a powder. Fill all of the window spaces with the
ground candy and bake 4 to 5 minutes until the powder melts into smooth
translucent panes. Cool completely before removing from baking sheet.

2 Fill a pastry bag fitted with a round tip with white royal icing. Pipe window-
panes, shutters, and a door. Set aside to dry, about 30 minutes.

assemble cottage

1 Cut a 2-inch hole in the cardboard circle and set aside. Replace the round
tip with a medium star tip. Pipe a line of icing along one edge of the front
of the gingerbread cottage. Do not pipe along slanted roof edge. Stand the
front piece 1 1/2 inches from the edge of the cardboard circle base. Fit
a side piece against the edge of the front piece. Hold the gingerbread in
place until the two pieces adhere to one another. Repeat for the second side.

2 Pipe icing along the inner side edges of the back piece of the cottage and
fit it against the two open sides. Adjust the alignment and let the icing set
for 30 minutes. Pipe along the slanted edges and set the roof pieces on
the structure. Allow the icing to set until it's completely dry.

decorate cottage

1 Fit a pastry bag with the small star tip and fill with green icing. Form bushes,
wreath, and trees by piping clusters of tiny rosettes.

2 Fit a pastry bag with a round tip and fill it with red icing. Pipe tiny dots of icing to mimic berries on the bushes, wreath, and trees. Change the tip to a medium star and pipe decorative swirls down the cottage corners and slanted roof edges to cover the white adhesive icing.

3 Using a small offset or icing spatula, spread white icing over one side of the roof, dripping some along the bottom edge to create icicles. Sprinkle with sugar crystals. Repeat for the other side. Pipe a straight line along the roof's peak and attach the candy canes. With the spatula, spread more of the white icing over the entire base to create snow and drifts.

4 Allow the cottage to dry overnight. Insert the light through the hole in the cardboard base and display the cottage lit.

gingerbread templates

Enlarge the templates with a photocopier to the desired size. Cut two roof panels (1) and two side panels (4) for each house.

1.

2.

3.

4.

paper doves

photograph, page 27

gift bags

photograph, page 87

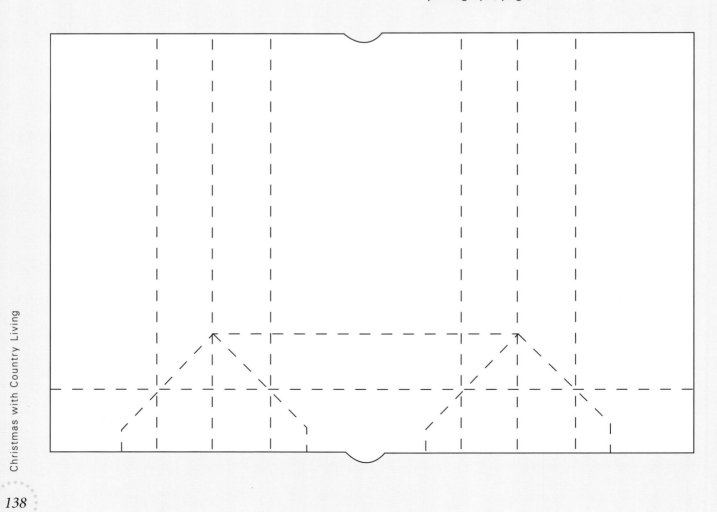

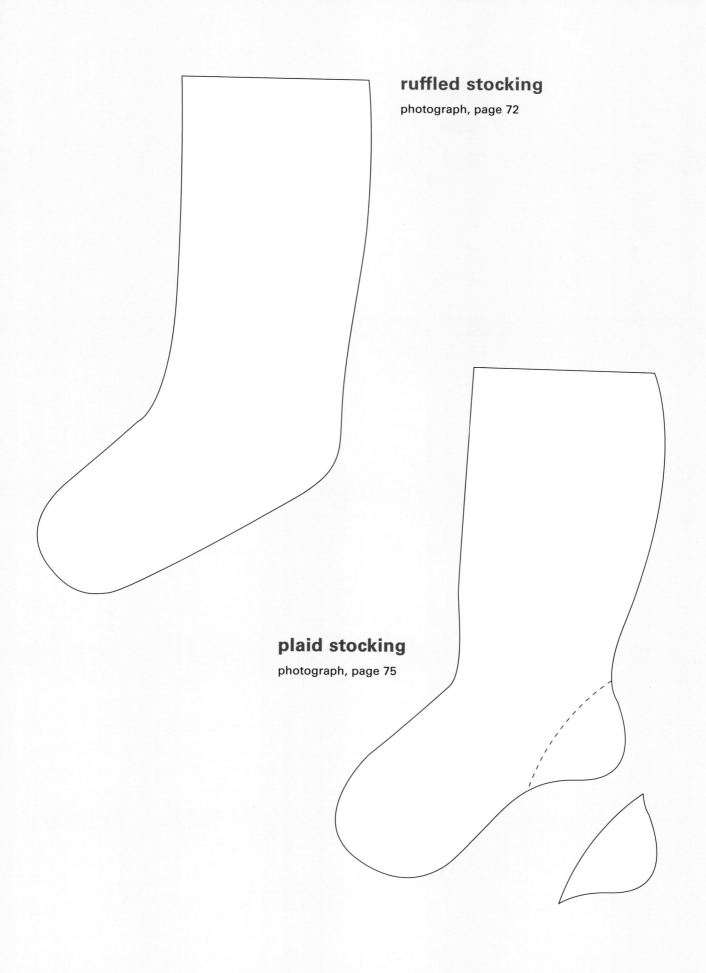

ruffled stocking

photograph, page 72

plaid stocking

photograph, page 75

Here is a chapter-by-chapter listing of sources for as many of the items pictured in the book as possible. We've tried to ensure the accuracy of addresses, telephone numbers, and Websites, but these may change prior to or after publication.

Decorating with Ornaments

Pages 17 and 18

Cherry table from Daniel Mack Rustic Furnishings, 14 Welling Avenue, Warwick, NY 10990; (914) 986-7293 or www.danielmack.com.

"Sissy" compote, "Athena" champagne flute, and "Stella" goblet from William Yeoward Crystal, (800) 818-8484 or www.williamyeowardcrystal.com.

"Vieux Paris" silver-plated flatware from the Blachere Group, (800) 641-4808 or www.blachere.com.

Glass birds and burgundy angel tree topper from The Merck Family's Old World Christmas, P.O. Box 8000, Spokane, WA 99203; (800) 962-7669 or www.oldworldchristmas.com.

Glass garlands from Kurt S. Adler, 1107 Broadway, New York, NY 10010; (212) 924-0900.

Glass balls from Christmas By Krebs, P.O. Box 5730, Roswell, NM 88202; (505) 624-2882 or www.christmasbykrebs.com.

Linen napkins and tablecloth from Laura Fisher/Antique Quilts & Americana, 1050 Second Avenue, Gallery #84, New York, NY 10022; (212) 838-2596.

Candlesticks from Tudor Rose Antiques, 28 East 10th Street, New York, NY 10003; (212) 677-5239 or www.tudorroseantiques.com.

Ribbons from C. M. Offray & Son, Inc., Route 24, P.O. Box 601, Chester, NJ 07930; (908) 879-4700.

Page 25

Red Stars from Midwest of Cannon Falls, (800) 377-3335 or www.midwestofcannonfalls.com.

Vintage crochet throw from Paula Rubenstein, Ltd., 65 Prince Street, New York, NY 10012; (212) 966-8954.

Ribbon from Ampelco, 1536 Brook Drive, Downes Grove, IL 60515; (800) 780-5830 or www.ampelco.com.

Fabric strawberries from The Prickly Pear, 54½ Skyhill Drive, Wolcott, CT 06716; (203) 879-6455.

Pages 26 and 27

Paper from Paper Access, 23 West 18th Street, New York, NY 10011; (800) 727-3701 or www.paperaccess.com.

Pages 28 and 29

Rag-ball ornament design by Amy and David Butler and Keith Keegan for Art of the Midwest, (740) 397-1236 or www.artofthemidwest.com.

Garland and wreaths from Laurel Springs Christmas Tree Farm, P.O. Box 85, Laurel Springs, NC 28644; (800) 851-2345.

Page 31

Felt garland from Morna Crites-Moore, (203) 938-8794.

Holiday in Bloom

Pages 36 and 37

Crystal compotes from Saint-Louis, (800) 238-5522.

Table sheer from London Lace, 215 Newbury Street, Boston, MA 02116; (800) 926-LACE or www.londonlace.com.

Garlands from Laurel Springs Christmas Tree Farm, previously listed.

Page 41

Fir balls from StoneKelly, 641 West 59th Street, New York, NY 10019; (212) 245-6611 or www.stonekelly.com.

Page 42

Cake stand from William-Wayne & Co., 850 Lexington Avenue, New York, NY 10021; (212) 288-9243 or www.william-wayne.com.

Pages 44 and 45

Garland and wreaths from Laurel Springs Christmas Tree Farm, previously listed.

Page 49 (top)

Peppermint pillows from Hammond's Candies, 4969 Colorado Boulevard, Denver, CO 80216; (303) 333-5588 or www.hammondscandies.com.

Page 53

Urns from Stanley & Grass, 166 Front Street, Marietta, OH 45750; (877) 878-2256.

Page 56 (top)

Pinecones from Mills Floral Co., 4550 Peachtree Lakes Drive, Duluth, GA 30096; (770) 729-8995.

Traditional Tartans

Pages 60 to 64

Tree, wreath, and greenery from Laurel Springs Christmas Tree Farm, previously listed.

Ribbons from C. M. Offray & Son, Inc., previously listed.

Pewter from Woodbury Pewterers, Inc., 860 Main Street South, Woodbury, CT 06798; (800) 648-2014 or www.woodburypewter.com.

Candles from Colonial Candle of Cape Cod, (800) 343-4534 or www.colonialathome.com.

Fabric from Flourishes, 200 Lexington Avenue, Suite 414, New York, NY 10016; (212) 779-4540.

Chair from the Lillian August Collection by Drexel Heritage Furniture, (828) 433-3200.

Pillows on chair from Shyam Ahuja, 201 East 56th Street, New York, NY 10022; (212) 644-5910.

Ottoman from the Chris Madden Collection by Bassett Furniture, (276) 629-6000 or www.bassettfurniture.com.

Tree ornaments by Tag, (773) 697-6300.

Pages 68 and 69

Evergreens from Laurel Springs Christmas Tree Farm, previously listed.

Wing chair from Circa Antiques and Design, 19 Main Street, Rockport, ME 04856; (207) 236-7404.

Gold-dust balls from Mills Floral Co., 4550 Peachtree Lakes Drive, Duluth, GA 30096; (770) 729-8995.

Pom-pom garland from Conso Products Co., (800) 845-2431.

Flocked gold balls from Midwest of Cannon Falls, (800) 377-3335 or www.midwestofcannonfalls.com.

Pages 70, 71, and 75

Plaid fabrics and red velvet from Beckenstein Fabrics, 4 West 20th Street, New York, NY 10011; (212) 366-5142.

Gilded Wrappings

Pages 80 and 81

Antique stool from Riverbank Antiques & Interiors, 169 West Front Street, Red Bank, NJ 07701; (732) 842-5400.

White quilt chain garland from Mama's Attic, 1910 Mosley Ferry Road, Chapmansboro, TN 37035; (615) 307-3180 or www.mamasatticonline.com.

White fabric candy cane from Cheswick Co., 10 Bluff Avenue, #115, Clinton, CT 06413; (860) 669-9121.

Silver and green stripe paper from the Nelson Line, 102 Commerce Drive, #6, Moorestown, NJ 08057; (800) 350-5463 or www.nelsonline.com.

Turquoise paper with silver stars by Glick Design available through Notes & Queries, (800) 783-8870 or www.nandq.com.

Silver-on-silver windowpane paper from Mani-G'Raps & Co., (800) 510-RAPS or www.mani-g-raps.com.

Metallic tinsel #01997PMB in silver from Plus Mark, (800) 251-0374.

Table from GB Home, 160 Monmouth Street, Red Bank, NJ 07701; (732) 345-0776 or www.cottagefabulous.com.

Pages 80 and 81, continued

Soaps from Rancé, available through Es'Scents International Inc., 7087 Commerce Circle, Suite C, Pleasanton, CA 94588; (888) 788-0768.

Ribbons from Ampelco Ribbon Co., (630) 620-5830 or www.ampelco.com.

Button spray from Laura Kent at the Red Bank Antique Center, Building 3, 226 West Front Street, Red Bank, NJ 07701; (732) 842-4336.

Gift card from Mira Aster, 55 Berry Street, Brooklyn, NY 11211; (718) 302-2420 or www.miraaster.com.

Page 85

Checkerboard rubber stamp from Hot Potatoes, 2805 Columbine Place, Nashville, TN 37204; (615) 269-8002 or www.hotpotatoes.com.

Page 88

Paper from The Jennifer Collection, 53 Second Avenue, Troy, NY, 12180; (518) 233-7218.

Ribbons from Midori, previously listed.

Strawberries by Cheswick Co., previously listed.

Pages 90 and 91

Metal flower wreath from Midwest of Cannon Falls, previously listed.

Greeting cards from Unusual Occasion Cards, P.O. Box 300748, Austin, TX 78703; (512) 474-2277; from Fred Flare Inc., 175 North Tenth Street, Suite 3, Brooklyn, NY 11211; (212) 675-4827 or www.fredflare.com; from Winters Ripp Design, 1133 Broadway, Suite 816, New York, NY 10010; (212) 367-8512or www.winrip.com; from Unique Artistry, 226 North Clinton, #327, Chicago, IL 60661; (312) 575-8665 or www.uniqueartistry.com; from SmART Blondz, P.O. Box 15044, Beverly Hills, CA 90209; (310) 273-2782 or www.smartblondz.com; and from Mimi's Papers, 38 Bruce Road, Montclair, NJ 07043; (973) 783-1511.

Bottlebrush trees from Backporch Friends, 227 Main Street, Valentine, NE 69201; (800) 595-5907.

Curtain from Bella Notte Linens, Inc., 20 Galli Drive, Suite E, Novato, CA 94949; (415) 883-3434.

Feather tree from Twins Feather Trees, (513) 681-9357 or www.twinsfeathertrees.com.

Ornaments from Janet Combs, 1200 North 64th Street, Waco, TX 76710; (254) 776-5724.

Furniture from GB Home, previously listed.

Chenille stockings from Apple Tree Mercantile by Patrice Brown, 311 West Fifth Street, East Liverpool, OH 43920; (330) 385-2304.

Armchair, sconces, and vases from Riverbank Antiques and Interiors, previously listed.

Medallion oilcloth from Oilcloth International, (323) 344-3967 or www.oilcloth.com.

Gift packaging from Midori, Mani-G'Raps, Laura Kent, the Nelson Line, C. M. Offray & Son, Inc., the Jennifer Collection, Notes & Queries, and Ampelco Ribbon, all previously listed, and Jillson & Roberts, 3300 West Castor, Santa Ana, CA 92704; (800) 233-0070 or www.jrgiftwrap.com.

Baby booties from City Cricket, 215 West 10th Street, New York, NY 10014; (212) 242-2258.

Christmas Breakfast

Pages 94 to 103

Linens from Trouvaille Française, (212) 737-6015.

Tableware from Tudor Rose Antiques, 28 East 10th Street, New York, NY 10003; (212) 677-5239.

Tableware from Guilford Forge, (800) 717-4135 or www.guilfordforge.com.

Intimate Gathering

Pages 104 to 109

Plants and pots from Smith & Hawken, (800) 776-3336 or www.smithhawken.com.

Greens from Laurel Springs Christmas Tree Farm, previously listed.

Candles from Colonial Candle of Cape Cod, (800) 437-1238 or www.colonialathome.com.

photography credits

Jim Bastardo
Front cover; pages 1, 60–64, 77, 78, 82, 84

Gordon Beall
Pages 15 (top), 39, 40 (bottom)

John Bessler
Page 20

John Blair
Pages 14, 32, 44, 45, 89

Monica Buck
Page 12

Gridley & Graves
Pages 56, 57

Gross & Daley
Pages 16, 17; back cover (top)

John Gruen
Pages 111, 144

Kari Haavisto
Pages 18, 19

Lisa Hubbard
Pages 124, 127–129

Paul Kopelow
Pages 22, 23

Charles Maraia
Pages 8, 80, 81, 88, 90, 91

Andrew McCaul
Pages 2, 6, 15 (bottom), 22, 23, 30, 48, 49 (top), 65, 66 (top), 70–75, 79, 85–87, 92, 93; back cover (bottom center)

Bryan E. McCay
Pages 34, 40, 66 (bottom), 67

Keith Scott Morton
Pages 4–5, 6 (right), 10, 21, 27, 28, 29, 31, 38, 43, 46, 47, 49 (bottom), 51–55, 58 (bottom), 59, 68, 69, 104–110, 112–123; back cover (bottom left, bottom right)

David Prince
Pages 7 (bottom left), 9, 13, 83, 126, 134

Steven Randazzo
Pages 26, 50, 58 (top)

William P. Steele
Page 41

Ann Stratton
Pages 7 (top left), 42, 94–103

Al Teufen
Pages 35–37